Harvard Business Review

ON

THE MIND OF THE LEADER

THE HARVARD BUSINESS REVIEW PAPERBACK SERIES

The series is designed to bring today's managers and professionals the fundamental information they need to stay competitive in a fast-moving world. From the preeminent thinkers whose work has defined an entire field to the rising stars who will redefine the way we think about business, here are the leading minds and landmark ideas that have established the *Harvard Business Review* as required reading for ambitious businesspeople in organizations around the globe.

Other books in the series:

Other books in the series (continued):

Harvard
Business
Review

ON

THE MIND OF THE LEADER

A HARVARD BUSINESS REVIEW PAPERBACK

The *Harvard Business Review* articles in this collection are available as
individual reprints. Discounts apply to quantity purchases. For information and ordering, please contact Customer Service, Harvard Business
School Publishing, Boston, MA 02163. Telephone: (617) 783-7500 or
(800) 988-0886, 8 A.M. to 6 P.M. Eastern Time, Monday through Friday.
Fax: (617) 783-7555, 24 hours a day. E-mail: custserv@hbsp.harvard.edu.

Library of Congress Cataloging-in-Publication Data
Harvard business review on the mind of the leader.
     p. cm. — (The Harvard business review paperback series)
     Includes index.
     ISBN 1-59139-640-9
     1. Leadership. I. Harvard Business School. II. Harvard business
review. III. Series.
HD57.7.H38735 2005
658.4´092—dc22   2004016505
                                                   CIP

Contents

Harvard Business Review

ON

THE MIND OF THE LEADER

Leadership—Warts and All

BARBARA KELLERMAN

Executive Summary

DOES USING TYCO'S FUNDS to purchase a $6,000 shower curtain and a $15,000 dog-shaped umbrella stand make Dennis Kozlowski a bad leader? Is Martha Stewart's career any less instructive because she may have sold some shares on the basis of a tip-off? Is leadership synonymous with moral leadership?

Before 1970, the answer from most leadership theorists would certainly have been no. Look at Hitler, Stalin, Pol Pot, Mao Tse-tung—great leaders all, but hardly good men. In fact, capricious, murderous, high-handed, corrupt, and evil leaders are effective and commonplace. Machiavelli celebrated them; the U.S. constitution built in safeguards against them. Everywhere, power goes hand in hand with corruption—everywhere, that is, except in the literature of business leadership.

To read Tom Peters, Jay Conger, John Kotter, and most of their colleagues, leaders are, as Warren Bennis puts it, individuals who create shared meaning, have a distinctive voice, have the capacity to adapt, and have integrity. According to today's business literature, to be a leader is, by definition, to be benevolent.

But leadership is not a moral concept, and it is high time we acknowledge that fact. We have as much to learn from those we would regard as bad examples as we do from the far fewer good examples we're presented with these days.

Leaders are like the rest of us: trustworthy and deceitful, cowardly and brave, greedy and generous. To assume that all good leaders are good people is to be willfully blind to the reality of the human condition, and it severely limits our ability to become better leaders. Worse, it may cause senior executives to think that, because they are leaders, they are never deceitful, cowardly, or greedy. That way lies disaster.

"WE TELL OURSELVES STORIES in order to live," Joan Didion once wrote, to explain the unfounded optimism human beings display. Good stories make the world more bearable. Inevitably, therefore, we want to tell—and be told—stories that make us feel better, even if that means that we don't get as complete a picture as we need.

People who study leaders have fallen victim to this instinct in a big way. In the leadership literature of the past several decades, almost all successful authors have fed into their readers' (and perhaps their own) yearnings for feel-good stories. Just reflect on some of the best sellers of the last 20 to 30 years: Thomas J. Peters and Robert H. Waterman, Jr.'s *In Search of Excellence*; Warren Bennis and Burt Nanus's *Leaders: Strategies for Taking Charge*; John P. Kotter's *A Force for Change: How Leadership Differs from Management*; and Jay A. Conger and Beth Benjamin's *Building Leaders*. Although a few authors have recently taken exception to the blind belief in the inherent goodness of leadership—notably Sydney Finkelstein in his book *Why Smart Executives Fail and What You Can Learn from Their Mistakes*—most of the hugely successful scholars argue, often with passion, that effective leaders are persons of merit, or at least of good intentions. It almost seems that by definition bad people cannot be good leaders.

If most leaders were worthy people, it would be easy to understand why we accentuate the positive. But the reality is, of course, that flawed leaders are everywhere. In corporations, overweening personal ambition and greed have driven many a CEO to run afoul of the law. In the last couple of years alone, scores of powerful and successful executives have been indicted for financial wrongdoing of various kinds. Think of Andy Fastow of Enron and Dennis Kozlowski at Tyco. Even homemaking diva Martha Stewart has joined the ranks of the indicted. As the *New York Times* wryly quipped, it now "takes a scorecard to keep up with corporate scandals in America."

Of course, corporations don't have a corner on the market in bad leaders. Politics is replete with the most extreme of examples. Hitler, Stalin, and Pol Pot come immediately to mind: all power-mad and evil but nonetheless highly effective as leaders. These extreme cases aside, stories about the failings of more reasonable public officials litter the newspaper headlines. Consider

Peter Mandelson, a member of Tony Blair's cabinet, respected both for his political skills and his understanding of public policy. In 1998, Mandelson was forced to resign from the cabinet after it was revealed that he had accepted an improper loan of £373,000 to help buy a swanky home in London's Notting Hill.

And, certainly, it doesn't end there. Accounts of the "wayward shepherds" in the Roman Catholic Church, as one journalist put it, continue to mount. To name just two of the highest profile examples: In 2003, a grand jury alleged that Roman Catholic authorities on Long Island, New York, had long conspired to protect 58 "rogue clergymen" from facing charges of sexual abuse. And in Boston, no fewer than 86 people filed civil lawsuits against John J. Geoghan, the convicted child molester who was later murdered in prison. Again and again, the suits alleged Cardinal Bernard F. Law, archbishop of the Boston Catholic Archdiocese for 18 years, returned Geoghan to parish work although Law had evidence that Geoghan repeatedly molested boys.

It is impossible to deny that bad or at least unworthy people often occupy and successfully fill top leadership positions, and it is high time leadership experts acknowledge the fact. For, contrary to the expectations of these experts, we have as much to learn from people we would regard as bad examples as we do from the far less numerous good examples we're presented with these days. Is Martha Stewart's career as a successful entrepreneur any the less instructive because she may have once sold some shares on the basis of a tip-off? Does Law's gross negligence on the issue of child abuse negate the fact that during his years in Boston he effectively managed to balance his traditional view of the church with progressive positions on discrimination and poverty? In the following pages, I shall attempt to explain how we came to accept such a skewed, moralistic understanding of leadership and in doing so I hope to put the warts—and the reality—back into the picture.

Leaders Weren't Always Nice

Although most contemporary scholarship is focused on leaders who are blemish-free, it was not always that way. Throughout history nearly all the great political theorists have recognized the reality of bad leaders, often accentuating the need to control their malicious tendencies. Influenced by religious traditions that focus on good and evil, and often personally affected by the trauma of war and internal disorder, political thinkers in former times took rather a jaundiced view of human nature.

Consider Machiavelli, a player in fifteenth- and sixteenth-century Florentine politics and often a witness to brutal warfare. Famous for his advice to political players in his classic book *The Prince*, Machiavelli outlined opportunities associated with forceful leadership. For most of us, coercive leadership almost by definition equals bad leadership. But as someone who was familiar both with the ways of the world and with the human psyche, Machiavelli argued that the only truly bad leadership is weak leadership. His philosophy was predicated on the assumption that some leaders need to use force to hold personal power and to maintain public order. Machiavelli, therefore, actually admired unscrupulous leaders who exercised power and authority with an iron fist. And in *The Prince*, he wrote with apparent calm about the occasional need judiciously to apply "cruelties": "When he seizes a state, the new ruler ought to determine all the injuries that he will need to inflict. . . . Whoever acts otherwise, either through timidity or bad advice, is always forced to have the knife ready in his hand, and he can never depend on his subjects because they, suffering fresh and continuous violence, can never feel secure with regard to him."

Like Machiavelli, the Founding Fathers of the United States had personal experience of bad leadership, and they thought about it a great deal. Indeed, they were some of the greatest students of leadership of all time. But their reaction to bad leadership could hardly have been further from that of the author of *The Prince*. They understood that leadership is easily corrupted and often malign, and therefore they went to extraordinary lengths to construct a constitution that makes it hard for leaders to accomplish much without the negotiated consent of their followers. Thus, in contrast to modern leadership experts who focus on how leaders can be more effective, the Founding Fathers looked for ways to rein leaders in, to ensure that leaders could act only after building a coalition of partners.

In *The Federalist*, for example, Alexander Hamilton dedicated an entire paper to exploring the differences between the proposed presidency and the distant, detested monarchy with which his American audience had struggled. The king of Great Britain was a dreaded hereditary monarch; by contrast, the American president would be elected for only four years. The king's position was sacred and inviolable, but the president could be impeached, tried, and, under certain conditions, even removed from office. In short, the U.S. Constitution was created to preclude the possibility that bad leadership could become entrenched. The very idea of checks and

balances grew out of the framers' suspicion that unless
the proposed government had a balance of power, then
power would almost certainly be abused.

We know this. How could we not, after the twentieth
century, with not just Stalin, Hitler, and Pol Pot but Idi
Amin, Mao Tse-tung, and Sloboban Milosevic? As the
late Leo Strauss, a professor of political philosophy at the
University of Chicago, bitterly put it in his classic treatise
On Tyranny, the tyrannies of the twentieth century are
so horrendous that they "surpass the boldest imagination of the most powerful thinkers of the past." Having
barely escaped the Holocaust, Strauss recognized what
our leadership experts seem to have forgotten: Capricious, murderous, high-handed, corrupt, and evil leaders
are effective and everywhere—except in the literature of
business leadership.

Where the Theory Went Wrong

To grasp how dramatically we have moved in our thinking on leadership from Machiavelli and Hamilton, it is
helpful to see how the words "leader" and "leadership" in
everyday language have acquired an inherently positive
bias. Consider Lawrence Summers's speech when he assumed the presidency of Harvard University in 2001: "In
this new century, nothing will matter more than the education of future leaders." Harvard's "Statement of Values,"
published in August 2002, picks up this same optimism
when it says that the university "aspires . . . to prepare
individuals for life, work, and leadership." In both cases,
the words "leader" and "leadership" have been transformed from their Hamiltonian sense. Of course, Harvard
is not alone in equating the word "leader" with outstanding human qualities. Yale president Richard Levin claims

that the university's goal is to become truly global by "educating leaders." As we have already seen, most popular books on business leadership also equate the term with good leadership, and many books on political leadership follow suit.

The start of the transformation of leadership into something overwhelmingly positive can be traced in part to James MacGregor Burns. A biographer of Franklin Delano Roosevelt, Burns is a Pulitzer Prize–winning historian and political scientist of impeccable repute. In 1978, Burns published *Leadership*, an analysis and distillation of what he had learned about the subject in his lifelong study of politics. The book had a major impact both because of Burns's stature and because it appeared just before the teaching and study of leadership began its rapid growth. In it, Burns differentiated between "leaders," who by definition take the motives and goals of followers into account, and lesser mortals whom he labeled "power wielders." Burns's position was uncompromising: "Power wielders may treat people as things. Leaders may not." Burns's definition of leadership continues to dominate the field. For example, in the 2003 introduction to his widely read book *On Becoming a Leader*, Warren Bennis restates the position he took when the book first came out in 1989: Leaders create shared meaning, have a distinctive voice, have the capacity to adapt, and have integrity. In other words, for both Bennis and Burns— and indeed for most of their colleagues—to be a leader is, by definition, to be benevolent.

At about the same time as Burns's book appeared, another group of leadership theorists, led by Abraham Zaleznik, a psychoanalyst on the faculty of Harvard Business School, started to draw a distinction between "leaders" and "managers." In this construction, the leader is an inspirational and aspirational figure, while the manager handles the duller tasks of administration and maintains organizational discipline. But by casting the leader in such a heroic light, these leadership theorists only strengthened the confusion between leadership and goodness.

Business gurus were as much responding to market forces as propounding a new doctrine. During the last 25 years, the leadership field developed primarily in response to the needs of American corporations, which by the mid-1970s were running into trouble. As Rosabeth Moss Kanter put it in her book *The Change Masters*, published in 1983, "Not long ago, American companies seemed to control the world in which they operated." Now, she said, they are in a much scarier place, in which the control of oil by OPEC, foreign competition (then primarily from Japan), inflation, and regulation "disturb the smooth workings of corporate machines and threaten to overwhelm us." In response to this growing concern, American companies turned to business schools for concrete help in fixing what was wrong, and it is around this time that the leadership industry may be said to have begun in earnest. In 1982, funds were pledged to Harvard Business School to endow the Konosuke Matsushita Professor of Leadership, and there are now similar leadership chairs at other universities, including Columbia and the University of Michigan.

The fact that the contemporary leadership field is an American product—an American seed planted in American soil and harvested by American scholars, educators, and consultants—has profound implications for how we understand leaders. For one thing, current views of leaders have taken on aspects of the American national character. In particular, the positive thinking that infuses our national spirit finds its way into our leadership training. So, too, does the American dedication to self-improvement. Almost without exception, America's most popular leaders have personified this sense of possibility. Ronald Reagan captured the sentiment during one of the 1980 presidential debates. Evoking Thomas Paine and John Winthrop, he declared: "I believe . . . together we can begin the world over again. We can meet our destiny—and that destiny is to build a land here that will be, for all mankind, a shining city on a hill."

What We Can Learn from Bad Leaders

While the optimism of a Ronald Reagan can be highly inspirational—and even effective—as Reagan's own presidency showed, it can also lead to simplistic ideas about who leaders are and what they can do. Reagan himself provides us with many examples. Biographer Lou Cannon pointed out one: "The president was so cut off from the counsel of black Americans that he sometimes did not even realize when he was offending them."

People can easily accept the idea that there are lessons to be found in success stories. But it's a mistake to assume that we can learn nothing from fallen leaders. Indeed, some leaders achieve great things by capitalizing on the dark sides of their souls. Richard Nixon—relegated by many to the realm of mere "power wielder" after Watergate—was able to inaugurate diplomatic relations with China by capitalizing on his famous paranoia. No one thought that a suspicious and obsessed Nixon would be soft on Communism! Even monsters can teach us something about how to lead people. Hitler, for example, was a master of manipulating communications.

Likewise, many a lesson can be learned from business leaders' blunders and even from their malfeasance. Take the case of Howell Raines, the former executive editor of the *New York Times*. In the last several years, no leader has fallen further faster than Raines, who was forced to resign after only 21 months on the job. According to popular analysis, Raines had to go because reporter Jayson Blair committed multiple transgressions on Raines's watch. Raines might have survived his trial by fire if only he had not had a reputation for being high-handed and callous. No one who worked for Raines loved him; some people even considered him tyrannical.

But in all the postmortems about what Raines did wrong, few people have stopped to ask what he did right. We can safely assume that a man like Howell Raines did not get offered the most prestigious job in American journalism without being prodigiously gifted. The fact is that Raines was one of the great talents in the newspaper business. He had experience and expertise (he won his own Pulitzer Prize), and he had a stunning record of accomplishment. Under his leadership, the *New York Times* won an unprecedented seven Pulitzers for its coverage of the issues relating to the terrorist attacks of September 11, 2001.

Someday, when the story is dissected more dispassionately, I believe that we will find something to learn from Howell Raines's failure. Raines was a man of first-rate functional talent—an excellent writer, accomplished editor, a man with an unparalleled news sense and knowledge of how to cover a big story. What he failed to recognize, it seems, is that expertise is only one dimension of leadership and can even be a misleading one. Rewarding only technical merit and ambition, as Raines did, leads to a distorted kind of management and a lack of checks and balances on the team.

Raines, of course, isn't the only fallen leader from whom we can learn. On June 4, 2002, Manhattan District Attorney Robert Morgenthau announced the indictment of former Tyco CEO Dennis Kozlowski for allegedly evading more than $1 million in taxes on purchases of fine art. It was not that Kozlowski needed to shortchange the government; in 1999, his total pay was around $170 million. Rather, it was that after a remarkably successful run as a corporate leader, Kozlowski's impudence caught up with him.

Much has been made in the press of Kozlowski's lavish purchases—his $6,000 shower curtain, $17,000 traveling toilette box, $1,650 appointment book, and his $15,000 dog-shaped umbrella stand. But there was another side to the man. For in addition to throwing a multimillion-dollar birthday party for his wife on company money, Kozlowski was a very gifted CEO whom businesspeople once talked about as a second Jack Welch. Since 1992, Kozlowski oversaw an ambitious campaign in which Tyco acquired more than $50 billion in new businesses. Indeed, the habit of successfully swallowing up companies landed Kozlowski on the cover of several business magazines, one of which dubbed him "The Most Aggressive CEO."

As with Raines, Kozlowski's strengths and weaknesses were inextricably linked. A leader who was driven by a high-stakes mentality, Kozlowski showed almost no fear when taking enormous risks, a tactic that often paid off in his acquisition strategy. But that same mind-set led to excruciating misjudgments in his personal life, eventually ruining his career. Could Kozlowski have had the good side of leadership without the bad? Probably not, for most leaders have both. It is when they are unaware of their darker sides, and so fail to guard against them, that they fall from grace. Once again, the real problem is not so much that leaders have their dark side; rather it is that they—and everyone else—choose to pretend they don't.

Sᴄʜᴏʟᴀʀs sʜᴏᴜʟᴅ ʀᴇᴍɪɴᴅ ᴜs that leadership is not a moral concept. Leaders are like the rest of us: trustworthy and deceitful, cowardly and brave, greedy and generous. To assume that all good leaders are good people is to be willfully blind to the reality of the human condition, and it severely limits our scope for becoming more effective at leadership. Worse, it may cause the leaders among us to kid themselves into thinking that, because they are leaders, they must be trustworthy, brave, and generous and that they are never deceitful, cowardly, or greedy. That way lies disaster, for as we should all have learned by now, it is only when we recognize and manage our failings that we can achieve greatness—as people and as a society. Knowing that, then we can begin to explore the more interesting questions of leadership: Why do leaders behave badly? Why do followers follow bad leaders? How can bad leadership be slowed or even stopped?

Originally published in January 2004
Reprint R0401C

The Seven Ages of the Leader

WARREN G. BENNIS

Executive Summary

LEADERS GO THROUGH MANY transitions in their careers. Each brings new crises and challenges—from taking over a damaged organization to having to fire somebody to passing the baton to the next generation. These moments can be wrenching—and can threaten your confidence—but they're also predictable. Knowing what to expect can help you get through and perhaps emerge stronger.

In this engaging article, Warren G. Bennis, professor and founding chairman of the University of Southern California's Leadership Institute, reflects on leadership, recounting his own experiences as a young lieutenant in the infantry in World War II, as the new president of a university, and as the mentor to a unique nursing student. Bennis also describes the experiences of other leaders he has known throughout his career.

15

Drawing on more than 50 years of academic research and business expertise—and borrowing from Shakespeare's seven ages of man—Bennis says the leader's life unfolds in seven stages. "The infant executive" seeks to recruit a mentor for guidance. "The schoolboy" must learn how to do the job in public, subjected to unsettling scrutiny of every word and act. "The lover with a woeful ballad" struggles with the tsunami of problems every organization presents. "The bearded soldier" must be willing—even eager—to hire people better than he is, because he knows that talented underlings can help him shine. "The general" must become adept at not simply allowing people to speak the truth but at actually being able to hear what they are saying. "The statesman" is hard at work preparing to pass on wisdom in the interests of the organization. And, finally, "the sage" embraces the role of mentor to young executives.

My initial plunge into leadership came during World War II. I was a lieutenant in the infantry, 19 years old, and scared out of my wits. My orders were to assume command of a platoon on the front lines in Belgium. I arrived in the middle of the night, when most of the men were asleep. The platoon had taken up residence in a bombed-out shell of a house. I was led into the kitchen by the platoon's runner, and he offered me a bench to sleep on. Instead, I put my sleeping bag on the floor, next to the rest of the men. Not that I slept. I lay awake all night, listening to the bombs explode. I was as green as can be and knew little about command—or the world, for that matter. When the others in the house began to stir, I heard one sergeant ask another, "Who's that?"

"That's our new platoon leader," the man answered. And the sergeant said, "Good. We can use him."

Without realizing it, without having any idea what was the right thing to do, I had made a good first move. My entry had been low-key. I hadn't come in with my new commission blazing. In fact, I pretended to go to sleep on the floor. As a result, without drawing attention to myself, I learned something important about the men I would be leading. I learned that they needed me—or, at least, they needed the person they would subsequently teach me to be. And teach me they did. Over the next few weeks in Belgium, my men, who had already seen combat, kept me alive. They also taught me how to lead, often by example. The sergeant who had greeted my arrival with approval became my lifeline, quite literally, teaching me such essential skills as how to ride through a war zone without getting blown up.

While few business leaders need worry about being blown up, my experience in Belgium was in many ways typical of first leadership experiences anywhere. I was coming into an existing organization where emotions ran high, relationships had been established, and the members of the organization harbored expectations of me that I was not yet fully aware of. My new followers were watching me, to see if and how I would measure up. Every new leader faces the misgivings, misperceptions, and the personal needs and agendas of those who are to be led. To underestimate the importance of your first moves is to invite disaster. The critical entry is one of a number of passages—each of which has an element of personal crisis—that every leader must go through at some point in the course of a career. Business school doesn't prepare you for these crises, and they can be utterly wrenching. But they offer powerful lessons as well.

Shakespeare, who seems to have learned more every time I read him, spoke of the seven ages of man. A leader's life has seven ages as well, and, in many ways, they parallel those Shakespeare describes in *As You Like It*. To paraphrase, these stages can be described as infant, schoolboy, lover, soldier, general, statesman, and sage. One way to learn about leadership is to look at each of these developmental stages and consider the issues and crises that are typical of each.

I can't offer advice on how to avoid these crises because many are inevitable. Nor would I necessarily recommend that you avoid them, since dealing with the challenges of each stage prepares you for the next. But knowing what to expect can help the leader survive and, with luck, come through stronger and more confident. And so first to the leader on the verge—Shakespeare's infant, "mewling . . . in the nurse's arms."

The Infant Executive

For the young man or woman on the brink of becoming a leader, the world that lies ahead is a mysterious, even frightening place. Few resort to mewling, but many wish they had the corporate equivalent of a nurse, someone to help them solve problems and ease the painful transition. Instead, the fortunate neophyte leader has a mentor, a concept that has its origins in Greek mythology. When Odysseus was about to go off to war, the goddess Athena created Mentor to watch over the hero's beloved son, Telemachus. The fact that Mentor had the attributes of both man and woman hints at the richness and complexity of the relationship, suggesting a deeper bond than that of teacher and student. In the real world, unfortunately, goddesses don't intervene and mentors seldom materialize on their own. While the popular view of mentors is that they seek out younger people to encourage and champion, in fact the reverse is more often true. The best mentors are usually recruited, and one mark of a future leader is the ability to identify, woo, and win the mentors who will change his or her life.

When Robert Thomas and I interviewed two generations of leaders for our book, *Geeks and Geezers*, we met a remarkable young real-estate and Internet entrepreneur, Michael Klein, who had recruited his first mentor when he was only four or five years old, as Robert and I wrote in our *Harvard Business Review* article, "Crucibles of Leadership." His guide was his grandfather, Max Klein, who was responsible for the paint-by-numbers craze that swept America in the 1950s and 1960s. The fad made Klein rich, but none of his children had the least interest in that business or any other. But little Michael did, and Max jumped at the chance to coach and counsel him, often in the course of long telephone conversations that continued until a few weeks before Max died. In effect, the older man served as a first-rate business school of one for his grandson, who became a multimillionaire while still in his teens.

It may feel strange to seek a mentor even before you have the job, but it's a good habit to develop early on. I was recruited as a mentor years ago while in the hospital for several weeks following a "coronary event." There, I had a remarkable nurse who seemed to anticipate my every need. We spent hours together, often talking late into the night. He told me of his ambition to become a doctor, although no one in his family in South Central Los Angeles had ever been to college. I was won over by his character and drive, as well as by the superb care he gave me. When he was ready to go to medical school, I did all I could to help, from putting him in touch with appropriate administrators to giving him a glowing recommendation. He had recruited me as skillfully as any executive headhunter and made me one of the first members of the team he needed to change his life. The message for the "infant executive"? Recruit a team to back you up; you may feel lonely in your first top job, but you won't be totally unsupported.

The Schoolboy, with Shining Face

The first leadership experience is an agonizing education. It's like parenting, in that nothing else in life fully prepares you to be responsible, to a greater or lesser degree, for other people's well-being. Worse, you have to learn how to do the job in public, subjected to unsettling scrutiny of your every word and act, a situation that's profoundly unnerving for all but that minority of people who truly crave the spotlight. Like it or not, as a new leader you are always onstage, and everything about you is fair game for comment, criticism, and interpretation (or misinterpretation). Your dress, your spouse, your table manners, your diction, your wit, your friends, your children, your children's table manners—all will be inspected, dissected, and judged.

And nothing is more intense than the attention paid to your initial words and deeds, as any first-time presidential candidate can tell you. It's said of psychotherapy that the first ten minutes between doctor and patient are the most critical, and studies show that friendships formed by college students during orientation are the most enduring. Social psychologists have found that we base our judgments of people on extremely thin slices of behavior. We decide whether we are in sync or out of tune with another person in as little as two seconds.

So it is with leaders and organizations. Your first acts will win people over or they will turn people against you, sometimes permanently. And those initial acts may have a long-lasting effect on how the group performs. It is, therefore, almost always best for the novice to make a low-key entry. This buys you time to gather information and to develop relationships wisely. It gives you an opportunity to learn the culture of the organization and to benefit from the wisdom of those who are already there. A quiet entry allows the others in the group to demonstrate what they know. And it allows you to establish that you are open to the contributions of others. It shows them that you are a leader, not a dictator.

In retrospect, I realize that officer-candidate school had prepared me for my small triumph in that roofless house in Belgium. Even as the officers tried to cram all the survival skills we would need into four months of training, they told us again and again that the combat-seasoned men under our command would be our real teachers, at least at first. The same holds true in any organization. In the beginning, especially, your most talented, most seasoned, most decent followers will be the ones that keep you alive.

When Steve Sample became president of the University of Southern California in the early 1990s, he did a masterful job of easing in. He went to the campus incognito at least twice, and during one of those visits he attended a football game and spoke to faculty members and students who didn't know who he was. Those visits gave him a feel for the campus as it really was, not how the most assertive of his constituents wanted him to see it. And during his first six months, he did not make a single high-profile decision. He knew that the important things to be done could be deferred until the faculty, staff, and students were more comfortable with him and their relationships were more stable. Major changes in the first six months will inevitably be perceived as arbitrary, autocratic, and unfair, as much for their timing as for their content.

However, it is worth noting that, no matter what your first actions are, you can influence other people's image of you only to a limited extent. The people who will be working under your leadership will have formed an opinion about you by the time you walk into the office, even if they have never met you. They may love you, they may hate you, they may trust you or distrust you, but they've probably taken a stand, and their position may have very little to do with who you actually are. The leader often becomes a screen onto which followers project their own fantasies about power and relationships. To some degree, all leaders are created out of the needs, wants, fears, and longings of those who follow them. Events that predate your arrival will also shape followers' view of you. In an organization that's been through a crisis—several rounds of layoffs, say—people are liable to assume that you're there to clean house again and may respond with either open hostility or flattery in the hopes of keeping their jobs. Others may see you as their savior because of the bad leadership of your predecessor. Your first challenge is to try not to take your new followers' assessments too personally. The second—and far trickier—challenge is to embrace the fact that certain elements of their assessments may be accurate, even if they put you in an unflattering light.

The Lover, with a Woeful Ballad

Shakespeare described man in his third age "sighing like furnace," something many leaders find themselves doing as they struggle with the tsunami of problems every organization presents. For the leader who has come up through the ranks, one of the toughest is how to relate to former peers who now report to you.

Shakespeare painted a compelling portrait of the problem in *Henry IV, Part II*. Before Prince Hal becomes Henry V, his relationship with the aging rogue Falstaff is that of student and fellow hell-raiser. For all Falstaff's excesses, he is often Hal's wise teacher, helping the future king see beyond the cloistered, narrow education traditionally afforded a prince to glimpse what his future subjects feel, think, and need. But when it comes time for Hal to assume his royal responsibilities, he rejects Falstaff, despite their having shared a sea of ale and the sound of "the chimes at midnight." Henry doesn't invite Falstaff to his coronation, and he pointedly tells the ribald knight, "I know thee not, old man."

Today's leaders would instantly recognize the young king's predicament. It's difficult to set boundaries and fine-tune your working relationships with former cronies. Most organizations, with the exception of the military, maintain the fiction that they are at least semidemocracies, however autocratic they are in fact. As a modern leader, you don't have the option of telling the person with whom you once shared a pod and lunchtime confidences that you know her not. But relationships inevitably change when a person is promoted from within the ranks. You may no longer be able to speak openly as you once did, and your friends may feel awkward around you or resent you. They may perceive you as lording your position over them when you're just behaving as a leader should.

I know of a young executive, let's call her Marjorie, who was recently promoted from middle management to head of the marketing department at a pharmaceutical company. One of three internal candidates for the job, she was close friends with the other two. Marjorie had already distinguished herself within the company, so it was no surprise that she got the promotion, even though she was the youngest and least experienced of the three. But the transition was much more difficult than she had anticipated. Her friends were envious. She would sometimes find herself in the awkward situation of attending an executive meeting at which one of her friends was criticized and then going straight to lunch with her. The new executive missed being able to share what she knew with her friends, and she missed their support. Her fellow executives had a more authoritarian style than she did, and some even advised her to drop her old friends, which she had no intention of doing. Her compromise was to try to divide her time between her new peers and her old. The transition was still hard, but she made a good early move: She had frank conversations with her friends, during which she asked them how they were feeling and assured them their friendships were important to her and would continue.

However tough it was for Marjorie, she had the advantage of knowing the organization and its players. The challenge for the newcomer is knowing who to listen to and who to trust. Leaders new to an organization are swamped with claims on their time and attention. Often, the person who makes the most noise is the neediest person in the group and the one you have to be most wary of, a lesson I learned more than 50 years ago from the renowned psychiatrist Wilfred Bion. At the time, Bion was doing pioneering work in the new practice of group psychotherapy. He warned his students: Focusing your attention on the most clamorous of your followers will not only anger and alienate the healthier among them. It will distract you from working with the entire group on what actually matters, accomplishing a common mission.

Knowing *what* to pay attention to is just as important—and just as difficult. In their efforts to effect change, leaders coming into new organizations are often thwarted by an unconscious conspiracy to preserve the status quo. Problem after problem will be dumped in your lap—plenty of new ones and a bulging archive of issues left unresolved by previous administrations—and responding to them all ensures that you will never have time to pursue your own agenda. When I arrived at the University of Cincinnati as president I was totally unprepared for the volume of issues that found their way to my desk, starting with the 150 pieces of mail I typically had to respond to each day. The cumulative effect of handling each of these small matters was to keep me from addressing what was truly important: articulating a vision for the university and persuading the rest of the community to embrace it as their own. It is at this stage that an inability to delegate effectively can be disastrous.

Newcomer or not, almost all leaders find themselves at some point in the position of having to ask others to leave the organization—firing them, to put it bluntly. This is always a painful task, if only because it usually devastates the person being let go and because the timing is never opportune. Facing you across the desk always seems to be the employee who's just delivered triplets or bought an expensive house. There's little available to guide leaders on how to do this awful business in a humane way; only remember that you have people's emotional lives in your hands in such circumstances as surely as any surgeon or lover does.

The Bearded Soldier

Over time, leaders grow comfortable with the role. This comfort brings confidence and conviction, but it also can snap the connection between leader and followers. Two things can happen as a result: Leaders may forget the true impact of their words and actions, and they may assume that what they are hearing from followers is what needs to be heard.

While the first words and actions of leaders are the most closely attended to, the scrutiny never really ends. Followers continue to pay close attention to even the most offhand remark, and the more effective the leader is the more careful he or she must be, because followers may implement an idea that was little more than a passing thought. Forget this and you may find yourself in some less dramatic version of the situation King Henry II did when he muttered, of Thomas à Becket, "Will no one rid me of this meddlesome priest?" and four of his nobles promptly went out and murdered the cleric. Many modern-day Henrys have mused along the lines of, "We should be looking at our technology strategy," only to be confronted a few months later with thick PowerPoint presentations and a hefty consulting bill.

Followers don't tell leaders everything. I know of an executive I'll call Christine who had a close working relationship with the rest of her group. The department hummed along productively until the day one of her top performers, Joseph, showed up at her door, looking uncomfortable. He told her he'd been offered a job at another company and was planning to take it. The timing was terrible; the group was headed toward a major product launch. And Christine was stunned, because she and Joseph were friends and he had never expressed dissatisfaction with his position or the company. Why hadn't he told her he wanted a new opportunity? She would have created a job especially for him, and she told him as much. Unfortunately, it was too late. The fact is, however close Christine and Joseph were, she was still in charge, and few employees tell their bosses when they've talked to a headhunter. And because Christine and Joseph liked each other and had fun working together, she'd assumed he was satisfied.

A second challenge for leaders in their ascendancy is to nurture those people whose stars may shine as brightly as—or even brighter than—the leaders' own. In many ways, this is the real test of character for a leader. Many people cannot resist using a leadership position to thwart competition. I heard recently about an executive who had been well liked by his bosses and peers until he was promoted to head a division. Then those under him began to grumble about his management style, and it wasn't just sour grapes. His latest promotion had been a stretch, and he may have felt, for the first time in his career, vulnerable. Shortly thereafter, his employees began to notice that he was taking credit for their ideas and was bad-mouthing some of them behind their backs. When confronted about his behavior, he seemed genuinely surprised and protested that he was doing no such thing. Perhaps he was unconsciously trying to sabotage those under him to prop himself up. But those who reported to him began to leave, one by one. After a year, his reputation was such that nobody wanted to work with him, and he was asked to leave.

In contrast, authentic leaders are generous. They're human and may experience the occasional pang at watching someone accomplish something they cannot. But they are always willing—even anxious—to hire people who are better than they are, in part because they know that highly talented underlings can help them shine. Many of the greatest leaders of our times, including the Manhattan Project's J. Robert Oppenheimer, Xerox PARC's Bob Taylor, and even Walt Disney, had healthy enough egos to surround themselves with people who had the potential to steal their jobs.

The General, Full of Wise Saws

One of the greatest challenges a leader faces at the height of his or her career is not simply allowing people to speak the truth but actually being able to hear it. Once again, Shakespeare proves instructive. In *Julius Caesar*, that brilliant study of failed management, Caesar goes to the forum on the ides of March apparently unaware that he will die there. How could he not have known that something dreadful was going to happen on that inauspicious day? The soothsayer warns him to "beware the ides of March." There are signs of impending evil that any superstitious Roman would have been able to read, including an owl hooting during the day and a lion running through the streets. And then there is the awful dream that makes Calpurnia, Caesar's loving wife, beg him to stay home. She dreams that his statue gushed blood like a fountain with a hundred spouts. Shouldn't that have been clear enough for a military genius used to amassing and evaluating intelligence? If not, consider that Artemidorus, a teacher in Rome, actually writes down the names of the conspirators and tries three times to thrust the note of alarm into Caesar's hand, the last time seconds before Brutus and the gang fall upon him.

Caesar's deafness is caused as much by arrogance as anything else, and he is hardly the only leader to be so afflicted. Like many CEOs and other leaders, movie mogul Darryl F. Zanuck was notorious for his unwillingness to hear unpleasant truths. He was said to bark, "Don't say yes until I finish talking!" which no doubt stifled many a difference of opinion. A more current example can be seen in Howell Raines, the deposed executive editor of the *New York Times*. Among the many ways he blocked the flow of information upward was to limit the pool of people he championed and, thus, the number of people he listened to. Raines was notorious for having a small A-list of stars and a large B-list made up of everyone else. Even if Raines's division of the staff had been fair, which it certainly was not in the case of now-disgraced reporter Jayson Blair, the two-tier system was unwise and ultimately a career ender for Raines. He had so alienated the vast majority of people in the newsroom who knew what Blair was up to that they didn't even bother to warn him of the train wreck ahead, and he refused to believe the few who did speak up. The attitude of Raines and his managing editor, Gerald Boyd, was that their way was the only way. When a distinguished reporter dared to point out an error Boyd had made, Boyd literally handed him a coin and told him to call the *Los Angeles Times* about a job. The reporter promptly did, quitting the *New York Times* for the West Coast paper.

But the episode most clearly recalls Caesar's situation in that Raines seemed genuinely surprised when he was forced out in the summer of 2003. He had no doubt read Ken Auletta's lengthy profile of him that ran in the *New Yorker* in 2002, showing that Raines was widely perceived as arrogant. And he should have been a good enough newsman to be able to tell the difference between acceptance and angry silence on the part of those who worked for him. Arrogance kept Raines from building the alliances and coalitions that every leader needs. When Blair's journalistic crimes and misdemeanors came to light, there weren't enough people on the A-list to save Raines's professional life. Authentic leaders, by contrast, don't have what people in the Middle East called "tired ears." Their egos are not so fragile that they are unable to bear the truth, however harsh— not because they are saints but because it is the surest way to succeed and survive.

I've mentioned the wisdom of avoiding major change in the early months in a new position. At this stage, the challenge is different, because leaders further along in their careers are frequently brought in with a specific mandate to bring about change, and their actions have a direct and immediate impact on an organization's long-term fortunes. Hesitation can be disastrous. However, you still need to understand the mood and motivations of the people already in the company before taking action.

I wish I'd understood that when I arrived at the University of Cincinnati in 1971 with a mandate to transform the university from a local institution into a state one—a goal that was by no means widely shared among the faculty or, for that matter, the citizens of Cincinnati. One longtime university board member had warned me to keep a low profile until I had a better grasp of the conservative community and the people in it were more comfortable with me. I chose to ignore his wise counsel, believing that broad exposure of the university and, by extension, myself would benefit my cause. As a result, I accepted an invitation to host a weekly television show. Worse, the title of the show was *Bennis!* The exclamation point still makes me cringe. I might have been perceived as an arrogant outsider come to save the provinces under any circumstances, but *Bennis!* guaranteed that I would be viewed that way. That perception (all but indelible, as early perceptions tend to be) made it much harder to realize my vision for the university.

The corporate world is filled with stories of leaders who failed to achieve greatness because they failed to understand the context they were working in or get the support of their underlings. Look at Durk Jager, who lasted less than a year and a half at Procter & Gamble. Critics accused him of trying to change the company too much, too fast. But what Jager couldn't do was sell his vision of a transformed P&G to its staff and other stakeholders. His very able successor, A.G. Lafley, seemed at first to back off from Jager's commitment to "stretch and speed," but in fact Lafley has been able to bring about change every bit as radical as any Jager spoke of, including going outside the company for new ideas, a reversal of P&G's traditional "invented here" philosophy. How did Lafley manage? "I didn't attack," he told *Business-Week*. "I avoided saying P&G people are bad . . . I preserved the core of the culture and pulled people where I wanted to go. I enrolled them in change. I didn't tell them."

Another model for doing it right is Carly Fiorina. She took over Hewlett-Packard with at least three strikes against her—she was a woman, she was an outsider, and she wasn't an engineer. And the person who chose to battle her was none other than the son of a company founder and thus tradition incarnate—Walter Hewlett. But Fiorina cleverly honored the company's illustrious past, even as she prepared for change, including the merger with Compaq. Her first annual report included a vision statement that starts with the word "Invent," paying homage to the pioneering spirit that created HP while simultaneously rewriting the "rules of the garage." She also appreciated the gravity of the threat presented by Walter Hewlett and systematically buttressed her support among the other members of her board. When the moment came, the majority of the members took action and removed Hewlett from the HP board. Time will tell how successful the Compaq deal will be, but Dr. Bion would have given Fiorina an A. She didn't overreact to Walter Hewlett—she didn't attack him, nor did she spend too much time trying to address his concerns. Instead, she stayed her course and kept the focus of all her stakeholders on what was truly important.

The Statesman, with Spectacles on Nose

Shakespeare's sixth age covers the years in which a leader's power begins to wane. But far from being the buffoon suggested by Shakespeare's description of a "lean and slippered pantaloon," the leader in this stage is often hard at work preparing to pass on his or her wisdom in the interest of the organization. The leader may also be called upon to play important interim roles, bolstered by the knowledge and perception that come with age and experience and without the sometimes distracting ambition that characterizes early career.

One of the gratifying roles that people in late career can play is the leadership equivalent of a pinch hitter. When *New York Times* publisher Arthur Sulzberger, Jr., needed someone to stop the bleeding at the newspaper after the Blair debacle, he invited Howell Raines's predecessor, Joseph Lelyveld, to serve as interim editor. The widely respected journalist was an ideal choice, one who was immediately able to apply a career's worth of experience to the newspaper's crisis and whose tenure was unsullied by any desire to keep the job for the long term.

Consider, too, the head of a government agency who had chosen to retire from his leadership position because he had accomplished all his goals and was tired of the politics associated with his job. When an overseas office needed an interim leader, he was willing to step into the job and postpone retirement. He was able to perform an even better job than a younger person might have, not only because he brought a lifetime's worth of knowledge and experience but also because he didn't have to waste time engaging in the political machinations often needed to advance a career.

The Sage, Second Childishness

As I've pointed out, mentoring has tremendous value to a young executive. The value accrues to the mentor as well. Mentoring is one of the great joys of a mature career, the professional equivalent of having grandchildren. It is at this time that the drive to prepare the next generation for leadership becomes a palpable ache. I wrote earlier of my relationship with a young nurse who had ambitions to become a doctor. Clearly, the young man benefited from our relationship, but so did I. I learned about the true nature of mentoring, about its inevitable reciprocity and the fact that finding and cementing a relationship with a mentor is not a form of fawning but the initiation of a valuable relationship for both individuals. My respect for my former nurse only grew over the years. When he graduated near the top of his class from the University of Southern California Medical School, I was there to watch.

When you mentor, you know that what you have achieved will not be lost, that you are leaving a professional legacy for future generations. Just as my nurse clearly stood to benefit from our relationship, entrepreneur Michael Klein was indebted to his grandfather, Max. But imagine the joy Max must have felt at being able to share the wisdom he acquired over a lifetime as a creative businessman. The reciprocal benefits of such bonds are profound, amounting to much more than warm feelings on both sides. Mentoring isn't a simple exchange of information. Neuroscientist Robert Sapolsky lived among wild baboons and found that alliances between old and young apes were an effective strategy for survival. Older males that affiliated with younger males lived longer, healthier lives than their unallied peers. Whether ape or human, individuals in a mentoring relationship exchange invaluable, often subtle information. The elder partner stays plugged into an ever-changing world, while the younger partner can observe what does and doesn't work as the elder partner negotiates the tricky terrain of aging.

When we compared older and younger leaders for *Geeks and Geezers*, we found that the ruling quality of leaders, adaptive capacity, is what allows true leaders to make the nimble decisions that bring success. Adaptive capacity is also what allows some people to transcend the setbacks and losses that come with age and to reinvent themselves again and again. Shakespeare called the final age of man "second childishness." But for those fortunate enough to keep their health, and even for those not as fortunate, age today is neither end nor oblivion.

Rather, it is the joyous rediscovery of childhood at its best. It is waking up each morning ready to devour the world, full of hope and promise. It lacks nothing but the tawdrier forms of ambition that make less sense as each day passes.

Originally published in January 2004
Reprint R0401D

When Followers Become Toxic

LYNN R. OFFERMANN

Executive Summary

LEADERS ARE VULNERABLE, TOO. That is, they can be led astray just as their followers can—actually, by their followers. This happens in a variety of ways.

Sometimes, good leaders end up making poor decisions because well-meaning followers are united and persuasive about a course of action. This is a particular problem for leaders who attract and empower strong followers. These executives need to become more skeptical of the majority view and push followers to examine their opinions more closely.

At other times, leaders get into trouble because they are surrounded by followers who fool them with flattery and isolate them from uncomfortable realities. Charismatic leaders, who are most susceptible to this problem, need to make an extra effort to unearth disagreement and to find followers who are not afraid to pose hard questions. Organizational mechanisms like 360-degree feedback and executive coaching can help these leaders get at the truth within their companies.

Finally, unscrupulous and ambitious followers may end up encroaching on the authority of the leader to such an extent that the leader becomes little more than a figurehead who has responsibility but no power. There's not much leaders can do to completely guard against a determined corporate Iago, but those who communicate and live by a positive set of values will find themselves better protected. And since followers tend to model themselves after their leaders, the straightforward leader is less likely to have manipulative followers.

In this article, George Washington University professor Lynn Offermann explores each of these dynamics in depth, arguing that leaders need to stir debate, look for friends who can deliver bad news, and communicate and act on a solid set of values.

Douglas macarthur once said, "A general is just as good or just as bad as the troops under his command make him." Almost as he made that remark, his country's president was proving the point. For in late 1961, John F. Kennedy, bowing to pressure from his advisers, agreed to the escalation of American intervention in Vietnam. Among the advisers pressuring him was the senior author of a report recommending military intervention. And that adviser's trusted friend—an American general—was chosen by the president to lead the new U.S. command in Saigon. Given his loyalties, the general wanted to make sure things looked good on the surface, so he stifled evidence from the field about potential setbacks and obstacles in Vietnam, making it tough for the president to discern the truth.

That, according to author and journalist David Halberstam, was how President Kennedy and his advisers led the United States into Vietnam. The story starkly illustrates just how easily, and with the best of intentions, loyal and able followers can get their leaders into trouble. If an accomplished politician like Kennedy could be misled in this way, it's no surprise that today's business leaders often fall into the same trap. No matter who we are, we are all influenced by those around us. Some of us are leaders, but we are *all* followers. Indeed, Ken Lay, the disgraced ex-chairman of Enron, may not be entirely wrong in blaming unscrupulous subordinates and advisers for his company's demise. As an executive coach to senior leaders in a variety of industries for more than 20 years, I've seen firsthand just how easily followers can derail executive careers.

How does it happen? In the following pages, I draw both on my experience as a consultant and executive coach and on decades of research in organizational psychology to describe when and why leaders become vulnerable to being led astray by their followers. In some cases, as the Kennedy story illustrates, effective leaders can end up making poor decisions because able and well-meaning followers are united and persuasive about a course of action. This is a particular problem for leaders who attract and empower strong followers; these leaders need to become more skeptical and set boundaries. At other times, leaders get into trouble because they are surrounded by followers who fool them with flattery and isolate them from uncomfortable realities. Charismatic leaders, who are most susceptible to this problem, need to make an extra effort to unearth disagreement and to find followers who are not afraid to pose hard questions. Charismatic or not, all leaders run the risk of delegating to unscrupulous followers. There's probably little they can do to completely guard against a determined corporate Iago, but leaders who communicate and live a positive set of values will find themselves better protected.

When the Majority Rules

Although many leaders pride themselves on their willingness to take unpopular stands, research has consistently demonstrated that most people—including leaders—prefer conformity to controversy. And the pressure to conform rises with the degree of agreement among those around you. Even if widespread agreement doesn't actually exist, the very appearance of it can be hard to resist.

One of the most striking pieces of evidence for this was a series of experiments conducted in the 1950s by psychologist Solomon Asch. Asch showed participants a vertical line and then asked them to judge which of three other lines was most similar in length to the test line. Participants who made judgments on their own chose the correct answer 99% of the time. Yet when other participants answered as part of a group in which fake respondents had been coached to pick a particular incorrect line, almost three-quarters of the unknowing participants made at least one wrong choice and one-third of them conformed to the group choice half the time.

It's worth noting that the participants conformed without any pressure from the fake respondents. Indeed, the fake respondents were strangers whom the participants were unlikely to see ever again. In workplace situations where continued interactions are expected and where there may be concern about possible loss of face, one would reasonably expect conformity to be even more marked. What's more, most business decisions are urgent, complex, and ambiguous, which encourages people to depend on the views of others. We should hardly be surprised, therefore, to find that the ethical and capable individuals who served on the boards of companies like WorldCom and Enron turned "into credulous, compliant apparatchiks more focused on maintaining collegiality than maximizing long-term profitability," as the *Washington Post* put it.

What happens is that leaders faced with a united opposition can start to question their own judgment. And they should question themselves—the reason that unanimity is such a powerful influencing force is simply that the majority often is right. In general, research shows that using social proof—what others think or do—to determine our behavior leads us to make fewer mistakes than opposing the majority view does. But as even the smartest leaders have had to learn the hard way, the majority can be spectacularly wrong.

One reason that even well-informed experts so often follow the crowd is that people by nature tend to be what psychologists call "cognitive misers," preferring the shortcuts of automatic thinking over considered examination. These shortcuts can help us to process information more quickly but can also lead to monumental errors. For instance, product designers may assume that if they like a product, everyone will. Yet the flop of Dell's Olympic line of desktop and workstation computers taught managers there that products must appeal to more than the company's own technically savvy workforce. As Michael Dell put it, "We had gone ahead and created a product that was, for all intents and purposes, technology for technology's sake rather than technology for the customer's sake."

Cognitive miserliness can be reinforced by culture. In the United States, for instance, Americans have long tolerated—even encouraged—people who form and express quick opinions. It is not a reflective society. Americans like to brainstorm and move on. That shortcut mentality can be particularly dangerous if the opinions are presented publicly, because people will then advance their views tenaciously.

In such public forums, it falls to the leader to push followers to examine their opinions more closely. Alfred P. Sloan, the former chairman of GM, understood this very well. He once said at the close of an executive meeting: "Gentlemen, I take it we are all in complete agreement on the decision here. I propose we postpone further discussion until our next meeting to give ourselves time to develop disagreement and perhaps gain some understanding of what the decision is all about."

Another factor contributing to the power of the majority is that leaders worry about undermining their employees' commitment. This is a reasonable concern. Leaders do need to be careful about spending their political capital, and overruling employees one too many times can demotivate them. Indeed, there are times when going along with the majority to win commitment is more important than making the "right" decision. (For more on when it's wise to go along with the majority, see "Joining the Opposition" at the end of this article.) But other times, leaders need to listen instead to the single, shy voice in the background, or even to their own internal doubts. As Rosalynn Carter once said, "A leader takes people where they want to go. A great leader takes people where they don't necessarily want to go but ought to be." In going against the tide, the leader will sometimes boost rather than undermine his or her credibility.

Fooled by Flattery

Being swept along by their followers isn't the only form of influence that leaders need to be wary of. Sometimes, follower influence takes the subtler and gentler form of ingratiation. Most people learn very early in life that a good way to get people to like you is to show that you like them. Flattery, favors, and frequent compliments all tend to win people over. Leaders, naturally, like those who like them and are more apt to let those they are fond of influence them.

For their part, followers think that being on the boss's good side gives them some measure of job security. To an extent, they're probably right; even a recent *Forbes* guide to surviving office parties recommends: "Try to ingratiate yourself. In this market, people are hired and kept at their companies for their personal skills." Indeed, a recent study indicated that successful ingratiators gained a 5% edge over other employees in performance evaluations. This kind of margin by itself won't get someone ahead, but in a competitive market, it might well tip the scale toward one of two people up for a promotion.

Everyone loves a sincere compliment, but those who already think highly of themselves are most susceptible to flattery's charms. In particular, leaders predisposed toward narcissism may find their narcissistic tendencies pushed to unhealthy levels when they are given heavy doses of follower ingratiation. Gratuitous ingratiation can create a subtle shift in a leader's attitude toward power. Instead of viewing power as something to be used in the service of the organization, clients, and stakeholders, the leader treats it as a tool to further personal interests, sometimes at the expense of others in and outside the organization. This happens as a leader starts to truly believe his press and comes to feel more entitled to privileges than others. People often cite Jack Welch's retirement deal as an example of executive entitlement gone haywire. The resulting furor drew public scorn for a long-standing corporate icon.

But one of the most serious problems for leaders who invite flattery is that they insulate themselves from the bad news they need to know. In her memoir, Nancy Reagan relates how then–Vice President George Bush approached her with concerns about Chief of Staff Donald Regan. Mrs. Reagan said she wished he'd tell her husband, but Bush replied that it was not his role to do so. "That's exactly your role," she snapped. Yet followers who have witnessed the killing of previous messengers of unwelcome news will be unlikely to volunteer for the role. Samuel Goldwyn's words resonate strongly: "I want you to tell me exactly what's wrong with me and with MGM even if it means losing your job." As more staff ingratiate or hold back criticism, the perception of staff unanimity, often at the expense of the organization's health, increases as well.

The rare individual who won't join an ingratiating inner circle of followers is typically seen as a bad apple by both the leader and her peers. Even when this perception problem is acknowledged, it is tough to fix. Despite widespread publicity after the 1986 space shuttle *Challenger* disaster about the dangers of failing to attend to negative news, NASA is once again facing charges of having downplayed possible liftoff problems just before the *Columbia* disaster. In both cases, engineers allegedly did not inform senior NASA executives of safety concerns;

they either withheld information or presented it in ways that diminished its importance or feasibility. Obviously, this tendency to withhold information is not limited to government agencies. Bill Ford, the new CEO of Ford Motor Company, believes that isolation at the top has been a big problem at Ford—a problem he has spent considerable time trying to rectify by a variety of means, including forcing debate and discussion among executives and having informal, impromptu discussions with employees at all levels.

In dealing with ingratiation, leaders need to begin by reflecting on how they respond to both flattery and criticism. In considering a follower's advice or opinion, ask yourself if you would respond differently if a staff member you disliked made the same comment, and why. Are followers really free to voice their honest assessments, or are they jumped on whenever they deviate from your opinions? Bill Ford makes a point of thanking people whom he has overruled because he wants them to know that their honesty is appreciated. One simple test of whether you're getting the feedback you need is to count how many employees challenge you at your next staff meeting. As Steven Kerr, chief learning officer of Goldman Sachs, says: "If you're not taking flak, you're not over the target."

Organizational mechanisms can also help. Greater exposure to external feedback from clients, well-run 360-degree feedback programs, and executive coaching may be more likely to reveal the full truth. It's hard to lead from a pedestal; open channels of communication can keep a leader far better grounded.

For honest feedback, some CEOs rely on longtime associates or family members, people who may even take pleasure at times in letting some of the air out of the executive's balloon. (Your teenage children might particularly enjoy this, though they might not have as much insight into your business). Bill Gates, for instance, has said that he talks to his wife, Melinda, every night about work-related issues. In particular, he credits her with helping him handle the transition period when he turned over the Microsoft CEO title to his old friend Steve Ballmer. Ballmer, too, has been one of Gates's closest advisers. Gates says of this peer relationship with Ballmer: "It's important to have someone whom you totally trust, who is totally committed, who shares your vision, and yet who has a little bit different set of skills and who also acts as something of a check on you." And Gates's well-known friendship with fellow billionaire and bridge buddy Warren Buffett serves as a sounding board for both men. Disney's Michael Eisner had a similar relationship with Frank Wells, until Wells's death in 1994, with Wells enjoying the role of devil's advocate, challenging Eisner to ensure that the best decisions got made.

In his book *You're Too Kind*, journalist Richard Stengel gives an account of flattery through the ages, noting that "the history of how ministers have used flattery to control leaders did not begin with Henry Kissinger's relentless and unctuous toadying to Richard Nixon. . . . Cardinal Richelieu was a famous user of flattery . . . and he was a famous sucker for it himself." Stengel argues that corporate VPs who suck up to their bosses are no different than the less powerful chimpanzees who subordinate themselves to more powerful ones in the animal world. Though it may feel great at the time, stroking a leader's ego too much, and protecting him or her from needed information, can have negative consequences for both the leader and the organization. It's worth remembering the words of cartoonist Hank Ketchum: "Flattery is like chewing gum. Enjoy it, but don't swallow it." (See "Six Ways to Counter Wayward Influences" at the end of this article.)

Powers Behind the Throne

Caught between the Scylla of follower unanimity and the Charybdis of flattery, leaders might be tempted to keep their followers at a distance. But in today's world, this is simply not an option. CEOs of major firms cannot know everything about their own organizations. In coaching senior executives, I often hear them lamenting that they don't have full knowledge of what's happening in their companies. They report sleepless nights because they've been forced to make decisions based on incomplete information. They must rely on others for full, accurate, and unbiased input as well as for many operational decisions.

From the follower's point of view, this presents wonderful opportunities. He can learn and practice new skills as the leader relies on him more and more, and he may be presented with new opportunities for advancement and reward. At the same time, however, it opens the door for the occasional follower who uses his newfound power to serve his own interests more than the company's.

So how can leaders guard against that problem? They can begin by keeping ethical values and corporate vision front and center when delegating and monitoring work. Only then can they be certain that followers have a clear framework and boundaries for their actions. As Baxter CEO Harry Kraemer says, the key to ensuring that followers do the right thing is "open communication of values . . . over and over and over again."

Leaders can also protect themselves and their companies by setting good examples. Followers—especially ingratiators—tend to model themselves after their leaders. Thus, straightforward leaders are less likely to be manipulated than manipulative leaders are. And a leader who is seen to condone or encourage unethical behavior will almost certainly get unethical behavior in his ranks. Take the case of former WorldCom CEO Bernie Ebbers, who allegedly ridiculed attempts to institute a corporate code of conduct as a waste of time even as he pressed his followers to deliver double-digit growth. He shouldn't have been surprised to find that junior WorldCom executives cooked the books or at least turned a blind eye when others did.

Although competency is generally a good basis on which to grant followers greater influence, leaders need to avoid letting followers influence them based on competency alone. As W. Michael Blumenthal, former chairman and CEO of Unisys, once said, "When did I make my greatest hiring mistakes? When I put intelligence and energy ahead of morality." The danger here is that astute but unscrupulous followers can find ways of pushing their leaders in unethical directions and may even use the leader's stated values against him. Suggestions like "I know you like saving money, so you'll love the idea of . . . ," followed by a shady proposal, force leaders into the position of having to choose between eating their words and accepting the proposal.

At the end of the day, leaders have to rely on their instincts about people. Fortunately, there is good news in this respect. Research by psychologist Robert Zajonc suggests that we process information both affectively and cognitively and that we experience our feeling toward something a split second before we intellectualize it. If leaders are attentive, therefore, they may be able to tune in to a fleeting feeling that something is not quite right or that they are being manipulated before they rationalize and accept what they would be better off rejecting. For example, one tactic favored by manipulative followers is to create a false sense of urgency to rush the leader into an uninformed decision. Recognizing that you're being pushed too fast and reserving judgment for a time may save you from an action you may regret.

It's not only the people you delegate to that you have to watch, it's also *what* you delegate. Clearly, leaders can never delegate their own responsibilities without peril. Smart leaders understand that even well-intentioned followers have their own ambitions and may try to usurp tasks that properly belong to their leaders. Harry Stonecipher, now CEO of Boeing, likes to point to the great polar explorer Ernest Shackleton as an example of a leader who knew what responsibilities he could and couldn't afford to delegate. Stranded on an ice pack and crossing 800 miles of stormy seas in an open boat, Shackleton knew the deadly consequences of dissension and therefore focused his attention on preserving his team's unity. He was happy to delegate many essential tasks to subordinates, even putting one man in charge of 22 others at a camp while he sailed off with the remainder of the crew to get assistance. But the one task he reserved for himself was the management of malcontents, whom he kept close by at all times. Amazingly, the entire crew survived the more than 15-month ordeal in fairly good health, and eight members even joined Shackleton on a subsequent expedition.

B<small>Y UNDERSTANDING HOW</small> followers are capable of influencing them, top executives can improve their leadership skills. They can choose to lead by steadfastly refusing to fall prey to manipulative forces and try to guide the way toward more open and appropriate communications.

Followers, for their part, can better understand their power to inappropriately influence leaders. Once they recognize the danger they pose to their leaders—and ultimately to themselves—ingratiators may come to realize that isolating leaders from reality can be as costly to themselves as to the company's shareholders. Realizing the value of dissent may force followers to take more care in forming and promoting their opinions.

Understanding that some tasks are best left to a leader may help followers to know where to stop and leaders to know what not to give away. In the final analysis, honest followers have just as great an investment in unmasking manipulative colleagues as their leaders do.

Joining the Opposition

THE LEADER WHO AUTOMATICALLY rejects his followers' opinions can be as unwise as one who unthinkingly goes along with them. In fact, there are times when it is advisable to go along with followers who are plainly wrong.

A senior executive in the health care field recently faced a united front of followers in an acquired facility. The followers wanted the executive to retain a popular manager despite an outside consultant's report that strongly recommended the manager's dismissal. Staff members felt that the manager had been wrongly blamed for the unit's problems and that the unit had been mishandled, underfunded, and generally "done in" by previous management.

Although the senior executive was under pressure from her COO to dismiss the manager, she chose to keep and support him—and watch carefully. By choosing this course, the executive won the support and confidence of hundreds of employees who saw procedural justice in her willingness to give the manager a chance. With the full support of her staff, the executive then went on to lead a turnaround of the facility in short order, exceeding the COO's expectations. Indeed, the executive built so much credibility through her actions that she was eventually able to dismiss the manager, with the staff understanding that he had had a fair chance but had failed.

The executive recognized not only the unanimity of employees but also the importance of winning their buy in and commitment. She chose, intentionally, to defer to the staff's wishes in order to demonstrate her fairness and openness. After all, the employees could have been correct in their assessment. Even though that didn't turn out to be the case, the leader's considered decision to go along with her reports likely resulted in a better outcome than if she had summarily rejected their opinions.

Six Ways to Counter Wayward Influences

THERE'S NO GUARANTEED means of ensuring that you won't be misled by your followers. But adhering to these principles may help.

1. **Keep vision and values front and center.** It's much easier to get sidetracked when you're unclear about what the main track is.

2. **Make sure people disagree.** Remember that most of us form opinions too quickly and give them up too slowly.

3. **Cultivate truth tellers.** Make sure there are people in your world you can trust to tell you what you need to hear, no matter how unpopular or unpalatable it is.

4. **Do as you would have done to you.** Followers look to what you do rather than what you say. Set a good ethical climate for your team to be sure your followers have clear boundaries for their actions.

5. **Honor your intuition.** If you think you're being manipulated, you're probably right.

6. **Delegate, don't desert.** It's important to share control and empower your staff, but remember who's ultimately responsible for the outcome. As they say in politics, "Trust, but verify."

Originally published in January 2004
Reprint R0401E

Putting Leaders on the Couch

A Conversation with
Manfred F.R. Kets de Vries

DIANE L. COUTU

Executive Summary

MUCH OF THE BUSINESS LITERATURE on leadership starts with the assumption that leaders are rational beings. But irrationality is integral to human nature, and inner conflict often contributes to the drive to succeed. Although a number of business scholars have explored the psychology of executives, Manfred F.R. Kets de Vries has made the analysis of CEOs his life's work.

In this article, Kets de Vries, a psychoanalyst, author, and Insead professor, draws on three decades of study to describe the psychological profile of successful CEOs. He explores senior executives' vulnerabilities, which are often intensified by follower's attempts to manipulate their leaders. Leaders, he says, have an uncanny ability to awaken transferential processes—in which people transfer the dynamics of past relationships onto present interactions—among their employees and even in themselves. These processes can present themselves in a number of ways, sometimes negatively.

What's more, many top executives, being middle-aged, suffer from depression. Mid-life prompts a reappraisal of career identity, and by the time a leader is a CEO, an existential crisis is often imminent. This can happen with anyone, but the probability is higher with CEOs and senior executives because so many have devoted themselves exclusively to work.

Not all CEOs are psychologically unhealthy, of course. Healthy leaders are talented in self-observation and self-analysis, Kets de Vries says. The best are highly motivated to spend time on self-reflection. Their lives are in balance, they can play, they are creative and inventive, and they have the capacity to be nonconformist. "Those who accept the madness in themselves may be the healthiest leaders of all," he concludes.

Leadership is the global obsession. Thousands of recent books—many of them best sellers—have dissected the leadership styles of great leaders from Jesus to Jefferson. Business writers, too, have joined the frenzy. The trouble is, much of the business literature on leadership—unlike the broader literature on the subject—starts with the assumption that leaders are rational beings. In part, that's because readers come to these business books for advice, so they get suggestions on how to imitate the conscious motivations, behaviors, and choices of role models. Advice books are hardly likely to focus heavily on leaders' irrational side—and still less likely to suggest that the role models' successes may even stem from their psychological frailties. Yet irrationality is integral to human nature, and psychological conflict can contribute in significant ways to the drive to succeed. Surely, therefore, we can benefit from putting CEOs on the couch, to explore how their early personal experiences shaped subsequent behaviors and to understand how these leaders deal with setbacks and pain.

Although a number of business scholars—most notably Harvard's Abraham Zaleznik and Harry Levinson—have explored the psychology of executives, only one has made the analysis of CEOs his life's work: Manfred F.R. Kets de Vries, the Raoul de Vitry d'Avaucourt Chaired Professor of Leadership Development at Insead in Fontainebleau, France, and the director of Insead's Global Leadership Center. Kets de Vries is also a practicing psychoanalyst whose research has provided rich pickings: He has authored or edited some 20 books on the psychology of leaders and organizations, including best sellers such as Life and Death in the Executive Fast Lane, The Leadership Mystique, and The Neurotic Organization. Kets de Vries's work has brought him close to many of the world's leading corporations: The executives of such firms as Heineken, BP, and Nokia have drawn on his expertise. Indeed, it's probably fair to say that no other leadership scholar has had as much exposure to the mind of the business leader.

So it was to Kets de Vries that HBR turned for insight into what really goes on inside the mind of the leader. In this edited version of a wide-ranging discussion at his office in Paris, Kets de Vries draws on three decades of experience and study to describe the psychological

*profile of successful CEOs. He explores top executives'
vulnerabilities, which are often intensified by the ways
followers try to manipulate their leaders. Kets de Vries
also explains just how these vulnerabilities play out in
organizations and suggests how leaders might overcome them. His prescription for healthy leadership? Self-
awareness and a well-rounded personal life, as well as
an ability to suffer fools and laugh at yourself.*

**You've studied the psychology of leaders your whole life.
How do you identify the successful ones?**

The first thing I look for is emotional intelligence—basically, how self-reflective is the person? Of course, emotional intelligence involves a lot more than just being
introspective. It also involves what I call the teddy bear
factor: Do people feel comfortable with you? Do they
want to be close to you? An emotionally intelligent
leader also knows how to single people out and say, "Hey,
Deborah, you're special. I've looked a long time for you,
and I really want you to be part of my team." In general,
emotionally intelligent leaders tend to make better team
players, and they are more effective at motivating themselves and others.

Unfortunately, the right side of the brain—the part
responsible for more intuitive processes—is not stimulated in business school. As a result, few students work
to develop the skill of emotional intelligence. Furthermore, leaders do not always learn it on the job. This is
particularly true today as more and more CEOs come
from the financial sector, where emotional insight and
people skills are often underrated. Of course, over the
years, I've met highly successful executives who are not

self-reflective at all. They're total doers. You have to be a doer to make it in business; navel-gazers do not make great leaders. Nevertheless, in my experience, the most effective leaders are able to both act and reflect, which prepares them to manage for the long term. These individuals not only run, they also take the time to ask themselves where they are going and why.

Do the backgrounds of the successful leaders you've studied have anything in common?

There is evidence that many successful male leaders had strong, supportive mothers and rather remote, absent fathers. This is beautifully exemplified by Jack Welch, who, in his autobiography, describes his attachment to a powerhouse of a mother and depicts his father, a train conductor, as pleasant enough but not very present. The same was true of a very different leader—Virgin's Richard Branson, whose mother told everyone she knew that Richard would become prime minister one day. It was Branson's mother who convinced him that he could do whatever he set his mind to do; his father played a much smaller role in his life. Former President Bill Clinton is yet another product of an adoring mom and a missing dad (he died before Clinton was born). Indeed, it seems to me that there is a lot of truth in Freud's famous statement that there is nothing as conducive to success as being your mother's favorite. When it comes to women, though, it's harder to explain what makes for success—there still aren't enough women leaders in business for researchers to make any real generalizations. But it does seem that the model for great women leaders is more complicated than that for great male leaders. As with the men, some strong women leaders had powerful, supportive mothers. But others had powerful fathers. Indeed, a successful woman often has been her father's favorite son.

Would you say that culture plays a role in determining what type of leader you are?

Certainly, different cultures have very different expectations of leaders. In America, for instance, a leader is a big shot. He takes himself very seriously, and other people put him on a pedestal. In the Dutch language, however, the word for "leader" can have two meanings, one of which is "martyr." In other words, a leader is someone who suffers. To put yourself on display and blow your own trumpet would never be acceptable in the Dutch world of work (and otherwise). It would show exceedingly bad taste.

The link between leadership and culture is very complex. Let me approach it through a hypothetical situation, admittedly a difficult one. Imagine that you're in a boat with your child, your spouse, and your mother. It's sinking, and you're the only one who can swim. Who do you choose to save? When this question is posed across a spectrum of cultures, 60% of the respondents in Western Europe and America (men and women) say they would save the child, and 40% say they would save the spouse. In most Islamic societies, 90% of respondents (men only) say they would save the mother. Recently I was in Saudi Arabia giving a leadership workshop. In response to this question, 100% of the participants (all were male) said they would save their mothers. Officially, the logic here is that you can always remarry and have another child, but you can never have another mother. But psychologically, the fact is that women are not allowed to do much in

Saudi Arabia. They are very handicapped. So the only way they can live and get glory is through their sons (their daughters are also demeaned). What develops is an incredibly intense relationship between the mother and the son, so there is no wife—or child, for that matter—who can ever live up to the gratifications the mother provided.

This story has many implications, but to me it underscores the cultural complexity of leadership. It's not always easy to appreciate or understand that what people do, mean, and say varies from one culture to the next, and without that understanding, it is impossible to lead in another culture. A leadership style that would be effective in Sweden, for example, might be quite dysfunctional in Russia, whose business elite I have been studying for some time. Of course, I'm talking now about the national culture, not a corporate culture. But corporate culture varies enormously as well, and companies differ in how they regard factors such as power, status, and hierarchy. There are also great differences in the way executives from various national cultures look at control and authority. There are numerous explanations for this, but as the story illustrates, the differences often derive from variations in child rearing.

By the way, of all the national leadership styles I've studied, the Finnish is one I admire very much. Unlike the Swedes or the English, the Finns never had kings or queens except when they were imported, so they have this element of democracy and a strong belief that working hard makes things happen. The Finns also have a straightforward, plain honesty, which is very good in a leader. And unlike many American leaders, the Finns have a strong sense of humility. When things are going too well for them, they throw up their hands and groan,

"My God, the sky is going to fall down on us." That touch of creative paranoia can make for very good leadership.

You often write that executives are irrational. What do you mean by that?

If you study executives, you quickly see that they don't behave rationally all the time. Indeed, irrational behavior is common in organizational life. It was my realization of this—and my desire to understand that irrationality—that led me into the fields of psychiatry and psychoanalysis. Once I started, I found that business leaders were much more complex than the subjects most psychologists studied. People in mental hospitals are actually easy to understand because they suffer from extreme conditions. The mental health of senior executives is much more subtle. They can't be too crazy or they generally don't make it to senior positions, but they are nonetheless extremely driven people. And when I analyze them, I usually find that their drives spring from childhood patterns and experiences that have carried over into adulthood. Executives don't like to hear this; they like to think they're totally in control. They're insulted to hear that certain things in their minds are unconscious. But like it or not, people have blind spots, and the nonrational personality needs of decision makers can seriously affect the management process.

What are these blind spots, and how do they play out in the organization?

I'm struggling with a case right now involving an entrepreneur. Part of his problem is that he has great difficulty with authority. However simplistic this may

sound, his troubles really do originate in a difficult relationship with his father. On top of that, he had a mother
who was quite controlling. Not surprisingly, after he had
started his company, he had a very hard time delegating;
he micromanaged. For example, he opened all the mail
that came to the company, and he insisted that everybody's e-mails be forwarded to him! This level of control
was manageable as long as the company was in the start-
up phase, but once it had become a $20 million opera-
tion, the entrepreneur's lack of trust in others' capabilities had a stifling effect. Predictably, the entrepreneur
just couldn't keep good people. There was high turnover
as people bristled under his exceedingly rigid control.
Recently, this entrepreneur came to see me about hiring
a large number of MBAs. I'm sure I could find many
outstanding MBAs for his company, but I know they
wouldn't stay with him. They would surely cite different
excuses for their dissatisfaction and resignations, but the
real reason would be that the entrepreneur is a control
freak, a failing of which he remains largely unconscious.
And because he is unconscious of it, he can't take
responsibility for it, which means that nothing can
change. Unfortunately, I am inclined to say that even if
this entrepreneur could acknowledge his obsessive need
for control, he would most likely come up with many
elaborate rationalizations for his behavior. I believe it
would take a great number of interventions before his
destructive patterns could be brought to his conscious
awareness.

In my work with CEOs, I also find that many executives are trying to compensate for narcissistic wounds—
blows to their self-esteem that were inflicted in childhood by parents who were either too distant or too
indulgent. (A child in an extremely indulgent household

cannot develop a balanced sense of his own personality.)
Typically, people with narcissistic injuries have a great
hunger for recognition and external affirmation. To combat their feelings of helplessness and lack of self-worth,
they are always in search of an admiring audience. In my
work with leaders, I have found that CEOs generally have
no idea that narcissistic wounds underlie their behavior.
To make executives aware of their vulnerabilities, I
sometimes ask them to describe the most critical negative voice that still plays in their heads from childhood.
Even highly successful executives admit to saying things
to themselves like, "You're not as good as you pretend to
be. You're an imposter." This is a parental voice that has
lingered into adulthood. Larry Ellison is a very good
example. I never met the man, but I once wrote a case
about him. I found out that his stepfather used to tell
him repeatedly: "You'll never amount to anything. You
will never be a success." Of course, this affects his leadership style today. Ellison is always trying to prove the bas-
tards wrong. Not surprisingly, he has created a very
aggressive organization. In organizations, we often find
strong links between the personality of the leader, his
leadership style, and the general culture—especially in
companies where power is centralized.

*Can you expand on the narcissism of leaders? There's
been a lot of talk about the subject lately. Why is it so
problematic?*

We need to be careful here. Narcissism has a terrible reputation, often rightly so. But all people—especially leaders—need a healthy dose of narcissism in order to survive. It's the engine that drives leadership. Assertiveness,
self-confidence, tenacity, and creativity just can't exist

without it. But once a narcissist gets into a position of leadership, funny things start to happen. Because narcissistic leaders are often charismatic, employees start to project their own grandiose fantasies onto the narcissistic leader. And suddenly everything becomes surreal.

I remember being in a meeting once in southern Europe. Thirty senior executives were gathered for a presentation about the future of the organization. The president was a very wealthy man who used to brag that he would need ten lifetimes to spend all his money. Not surprisingly, his office was filled with enormous statues and paintings of himself. He arrived 20 minutes late for the meeting, and he came in talking on a mobile phone. Nobody acted annoyed. Eventually the presentation started, and the CEO's phone rang. He picked it up and talked for 15 minutes while everybody sat there, waiting. Suddenly the CEO got up and said he had to go. This was the most important meeting of the year, and he just walked out. But no one, not one person, objected. Everyone told him what he wanted to hear. It was as if the CEO were in a hall of mirrors.

This reaction on the part of followers is hardly unusual. Do you remember the Peter Sellers film *Being There?* It looks at the life of an illiterate and slow-witted gardener named Chance, who is standing in the street one day when a limousine backs into him. Hoping to avoid publicity, the woman in the car takes Chance home to be seen by a doctor who is caring for her husband, a big-shot financier and friend of the president. When the president asks Chance what he thinks about the economy, the poor man hasn't a clue. Taking refuge in what he knows best—gardening—he says: "As long as the roots are not severed, all is well." The president interprets this simple statement as a great revelation. The results are inevitable: Chance is eventually pushed to run for the presidency. It was George Bernard Shaw who said, "Kings are not born: They are made by artificial hallucination." There's a lot of truth to that. The problem with many so-called narcissistic leaders is that they both deliberately and inadvertently activate the latent narcissism of their followers. These followers are often ideal-hungry personalities who idealize wildly and uncritically. And if the leader happens to like being positively mirrored by others, he can become addicted to the followers' idealization of him. Tragically, some leaders get to the point where they fire individuals who don't praise them sufficiently.

Why are followers so prone to idealizing?

It has its roots in what Freud called transference. Transference is probably the most important concept in psychotherapy; it was one of Freud's great discoveries. After he started working with patients, Freud found to his great consternation that patients kept falling in love with him. To his immense credit, Freud realized that it couldn't be his own wonderful personality that was stirring up such deep feelings of admiration. Instead, he realized that in their dealings with him, patients were interacting with powerful figures from their own internal theaters, usually important childhood figures like parents, teachers, and siblings. Transference is the term for this continuity between early childhood and adult behavior. What Freud meant is that we all bring to our current relationships a map of past relationships that we transfer onto the present. This particularly happens during times of stress and in hierarchical situations, which are reminiscent of the parent-child constellation. Indeed, people in positions of authority have an uncanny ability to reawaken transferential processes in themselves and others. And these transferential reactions can present themselves in a number of ways—positively or negatively. One employee, for example, may relate to her boss as if he were her favorite brother, and thus she idealizes him. But that boss may relate to her as if she were his withholding mother! It is precisely this confusion of time and place that results in the psychic "noise" of the workplace. Sadly, Freud was not interested in business, so he never studied it. But it would have been fascinating to see what sense he would have made of everyone's tendency in business to relate to people as if they were someone else.

Doesn't all this put followers in a vulnerable position as well?

It certainly does. I discovered this when I was about 14 years old. I was with my brother in a youth camp in the Netherlands where we went every summer. Most children were sent to this camp for only three weeks, but we were sent there for the whole summer. After three weeks, there was always a transition between the old group and the new, and one year my brother and I decided to liven up the changeover with an initiation ritual. We placed a bathtub filled with freezing water in the middle of a field and announced that according to an old camp tradition, all the newcomers had to dunk themselves in the tub. I can still clearly remember more than 60 boys (most of them much bigger than us) lining up and, one after another, obediently immersing themselves in the cold water. Everything went well until the headmaster of the camp passed by. He was dumbfounded. He broke our spell by inciting the newcomers to rebel, pointing out that there were 60 of them against the two of us. Eventually, my brother and I got what was coming to us. But for me, the scene remained etched on my mind as a testament to just how far people are willing to go to obey what they perceive as authority.

The fact is that even scant authority can get away with murder, both literally and figuratively. Indeed, I would say that some organizations are so political and unsafe that they resemble concentration camps. Everyone kowtows to authority out of tremendous fear. And you can see why. I once met an executive who told me, "Every day I walk into the office, I can make the lives of 10,000 people completely miserable by doing very, very little." His company was probably not a very healthy workplace—why wouldn't he say instead: "By doing very, very little, I can make the lives of 10,000 people much easier"? That's why at Insead I try to introduce CEOs to a kind of applied psychoanalysis in an organizational setting. In each of my workshops, there are around 20 individuals who together might be responsible for 100,000 people. My hope is that by helping leaders to become a little more self-reflective, we can make their organizations a bit less like concentration camps.

But with all the psychic noise in organizations, how can leaders ever get honest feedback and criticism?

Today there is a lot of talk about using 360-degree feedback. I use it quite a bit in my leadership workshops. When I use it for coaching purposes, I gather information not only from people at the workplace but also from people close to the leader in his or her private life. This helps me get a sense of who the leader really is. But people at very high levels are usually considered much too important to go through 360-degree feedback. And even if they do go through it, they often don't get honest comments. That's because it's not very difficult for the person being evaluated to figure out who said what on the feedback forms. So the people giving feedback skew their answers out of fear of retaliation. But even if they did give genuine feedback, it's unlikely they could express it in a way that would pierce the leader's narcissistic armor. That's why I like to make the case for having an organizational fool.

What do you mean?

The fool I'm talking about is a foil for the leader—and every leader needs one. Down through the ages, the fool has played a traditional role as the stabilizer of kings and queens (and other leaders). This is the wise fool of *King Lear*—the guardian of reality. The fool shows the leader his reflection and reminds him of the transience of power. He uses antics and humor to prevent foolish action and groupthink. Let's not forget: Humor humbles. It creates insights. That makes it a very powerful instrument for change. Let me explain the importance of the fool through an anecdote. A couple goes to a fair where there's a large, impressive-looking machine. The husband puts in a coin and receives a card telling him his age and what kind of person he is. He reads it and gets excited. It says: "You're brilliant and charming. Women fall all over you." His wife grabs the card from him and turns it over. "Aha!" she says, "they got your age wrong, too." Leaders in all organizations need someone like this who is willing to speak out and tell the leader how things really are. That's precisely the role of the fool. He offers the king a delicious sandwich, and between the slices of bread he shoves in a little piece of reality.

To be effective, organizations need people with a healthy disrespect for the boss—people who feel free to express emotions and opinions openly, who can engage in active give-and-take. Sadly, this typically happens only after a leader is out of power. As former President George Bush once remarked when he was asked what had changed since he left office: "Well, for one thing, I no longer win every golf game I play." In a well-run organization, the CEO wouldn't win every golf game either. And if a leader wants honest feedback, he should ask himself whether or not he's created an organization in which there's a place for a fool.

You've often observed that leaders get caught up in a whirl of hyperactivity. What's behind that?

Anxiety is one reason. Action is a typical human response to anxiety, and executives tend to be an anxious bunch. At any given time, there are many things going on that the executives feel they have little control over. So, like anyone else, they tend to look for some form of support, and one well-accepted response in the business world is the retreat into action. Another reason is that many top executives suffer from depression. I see it all the time. The chief cause for executive depression is that people usually don't join the ranks of senior executives until they're middle-aged. And in middle age, people start to feel desperate about coming to terms with unfulfilled dreams before it's too late. The Germans have a term for this—*Torschlusspanik*, the panic that strikes because of the closing of the gates, the closing down of possibilities. Midlife prompts a reappraisal of career identity; it raises concerns about burnout and loss of effectiveness. By the time a leader is a CEO, an existential crisis is often imminent. This can happen with anyone, but the probability is higher with CEOs and senior executives, because so many of them have been devoting their lives almost exclusively to work.

I tell you honestly that very, very few executives lead balanced lives. They delude themselves about it, too. If you ask them how much time they spend with their wives and children, they give you numbers that are completely at odds with the numbers the families give. I worked for two years as a consultant and coach with about 150 managing directors of a large, well-known investment bank to help them be more effective as leaders in their organization. These were people who worked 70, 80 hours a week, and they worked very efficiently, very successfully. What's more, they were typically smart, pleasant, and insightful—very sure of themselves. But because they were such workaholics, these investment bankers were not secure about their personal lives. They had tremendous guilt over their families, whom they never saw. When I began my work with them, all they talked about at first was problems in the organization and conflicts they were having with one another. Eventually, however, as our conversations continued—often one-on-one—they began to acknowledge that the roots of their problems lay elsewhere, in some internal conflicts.

As I dug around, I found that these investment bankers, like many top executives who are obsessed with work and money, often had experienced deprivation of some kind early in life. They work for large salaries and option packages as a way of obtaining what is sometimes crudely described as "fuck you money," to be independent. It is their way of having more control over a world they often perceive (given their early experiences in life) as uncontrollable. The trouble is that once they've proved they're successful, they can't get off the treadmill. All they know how to do is work. In the meantime, their personal relationships have become a mess. So they feel stuck and bored, and that makes them more depressed. Unfortunately, in business you are not allowed to show pain. So to liven himself up a bit, the CEO might find a new wife, a trophy wife. Or he might try to pull off some really big, aggressive deal, like a takeover. Now *that* provides some excitement. What better way to cure boredom than by becoming a modern day Viking, raping and plundering? Mergers and marriages both help to mask CEOs' psychic pain. But at some point, all leaders have to slow down. Retirement looms. When that happens, the depression that has never been resolved starts to become apparent.

Let's conclude by looking at the glass as half full. What makes a leader healthy?

Healthy leaders are able to live intensely. They're passionate about what they do. That's because they are able to experience the full range of their feelings—without any color blindness to any particular emotion. At the same time, healthy leaders strongly believe in their ability to control (or at least affect) the events that impact their lives. They're able to take personal responsibility; they are not always scapegoating or blaming other people for what goes wrong. Healthy leaders don't easily lose control or resort to impulsive acts. They can work through their own anxiety and ambivalence. As we saw earlier, healthy leaders are very talented in self-observation and self-analysis; the best leaders are highly motivated to spend time on self-reflection. Another factor is that healthy leaders, unlike the less healthy ones, have the ability to deal with the disappointments of life. They can acknowledge their depression and work it through. Very importantly, they have the capacity to establish and maintain relationships (including satisfactory sexual relationships). Their lives are in balance, and they can play. They are creative and inventive and have the capacity to be nonconformist. These are the things that are fundamental, but I would also hope (after having said all of this!) that we can accept that we need a little madness in our leaders, because I happen to believe that those who accept the madness in themselves may be the healthiest leaders of all. To quote Shaw once again, "We want a few mad people now. See where the sane ones have landed us!"

Originally published in January 2004
Reprint R0401F

Managers and Leaders

Are They Different?

ABRAHAM ZALEZNIK

Executive Summary

MANAGERS AND LEADERS ARE two very different types of people. Managers' goals arise out of necessities rather than desires; they excel at defusing conflicts between individuals or departments, placating all sides while ensuring that an organization's day-to-day business gets done. Leaders, on the other hand, adopt personal, active attitudes toward goals. They look for the opportunities and rewards that lie around the corner, inspiring subordinates and firing up the creative process with their own energy. Their relationships with employees and coworkers are intense, and their working environment is often chaotic.

In this article, first published in 1977, the author argues that businesses need both managers and leaders to survive and succeed. But in the larger U.S. organizations of that time, a "managerial mystique" seemed to

73

perpetuate the development of managerial personalities—people who rely on, and strive to maintain, orderly work patterns. The managerial power ethic favors collective leadership and seeks to avoid risk.

That same managerial mystique can stifle leaders' development—how can an entrepreneurial spirit develop when it is submerged in a conservative environment and denied personal attention? Mentor relationships are crucial to the development of leadership personalities, but in large, bureaucratic organizations, such relationships are not encouraged.

Businesses must find ways to train good managers and develop leaders at the same time. Without a solid organizational framework, even leaders with the most brilliant ideas may spin their wheels, frustrating coworkers and accomplishing little. But without the entrepreneurial culture that develops when a leader is at the helm of an organization, a business will stagnate and rapidly lose competitive power.

The traditional view of management, back in 1977 when Abraham Zaleznik wrote this article, centered on organizational structure and processes. Managerial development at the time focused exclusively on building competence, control, and the appropriate balance of power. That view, Zaleznik argued, omitted the essential leadership *elements of inspiration, vision, and human passion— which drive corporate success.*

The difference between managers and leaders, he wrote, lies in the conceptions they hold, deep in their psyches, of chaos and order. Managers embrace process, seek stability and control, and instinctively try to resolve problems quickly—sometimes before they fully understand a

*problem's significance. Leaders, in contrast, tolerate chaos
and lack of structure and are willing to delay closure in
order to understand the issues more fully. In this way,
Zaleznik argued, business leaders have much more in
common with artists, scientists, and other creative
thinkers than they do with managers. Organizations need
both managers and leaders to succeed, but developing
both requires a reduced focus on logic and strategic exer-
cises in favor of an environment where creativity and
imagination are permitted to flourish.*

W HAT IS THE IDEAL WAY TO develop leadership?
Every society provides its own answer to this question,
and each, in groping for answers, defines its deepest concerns about the purposes, distributions, and uses of
power. Business has contributed its answer to the leadership question by evolving a new breed called the manager. Simultaneously, business has established a new
power ethic that favors collective over individual leadership, the cult of the group over that of personality. While
ensuring the competence, control, and the balance of
power among groups with the potential for rivalry, managerial leadership unfortunately does not necessarily
ensure imagination, creativity, or ethical behavior in
guiding the destinies of corporate enterprises.

Leadership inevitably requires using power to influence the thoughts and actions of other people. Power in
the hands of an individual entails human risks: first, the
risk of equating power with the ability to get immediate
results; second, the risk of ignoring the many different
ways people can legitimately accumulate power; and
third, the risk of losing self-control in the desire for
power. The need to hedge these risks accounts in part
for the development of collective leadership and the

managerial ethic. Consequently, an inherent conservatism dominates the culture of large organizations. In *The Second American Revolution*, John D. Rockefeller III describes the conservatism of organizations:

> *"An organization is a system, with a logic of its own, and all the weight of tradition and inertia. The deck is stacked in favor of the tried and proven way of doing things and against the taking of risks and striking out in new directions."[1]*

Out of this conservatism and inertia, organizations provide succession to power through the development of managers rather than individual leaders. Ironically, this ethic fosters a bureaucratic culture in business, supposedly the last bastion protecting us from the encroachments and controls of bureaucracy in government and education.

Manager vs. Leader Personality

A managerial culture emphasizes rationality and control. Whether his or her energies are directed toward goals, resources, organization structures, or people, a manager is a problem solver. The manager asks: "What problems have to be solved, and what are the best ways to achieve results so that people will continue to contribute to this organization?" From this perspective, leadership is simply a practical effort to direct affairs; and to fulfill his or her task, a manager requires that many people operate efficiently at different levels of status and responsibility. It takes neither genius nor heroism to be a manager, but rather persistence, tough-mindedness, hard work, intelligence, analytical ability, and perhaps most important, tolerance and goodwill.

Another conception of leadership, however, attaches almost mystical beliefs to what a leader is and assumes that only great people are worthy of the drama of power and politics. Here leadership is a psychodrama in which a brilliant, lonely person must gain control of himself or herself as a precondition for controlling others. Such an expectation of leadership contrasts sharply with the mundane, practical, and yet important conception that leadership is really managing work that other people do.

Three questions come to mind. Is this leadership mystique merely a holdover from our childhood—from a sense of dependency and a longing for good and heroic parents? Or is it true that no matter how competent managers are, their leadership stagnates because of their limitations in visualizing purposes and generating value in work? Driven by narrow purposes, without an imaginative capacity and the ability to communicate, do managers then perpetuate group conflicts instead of reforming them into broader desires and goals?

If indeed problems demand greatness, then judging by past performance, the selection and development of leaders leave a great deal to chance. There are no known ways to train "great" leaders. Further, beyond what we leave to chance, there is a deeper issue in the relationship between the need for competent managers and the longing for great leaders.

What it takes to ensure a supply of people who will assume practical responsibility may inhibit the development of great leaders. On the other hand, the presence of great leaders may undermine the development of managers who typically become very anxious in the relative disorder that leaders seem to generate.

It is easy enough to dismiss the dilemma of training managers, though we may need new leaders or leaders at the expense of managers, by saying that the need is for people who can be both. But just as a managerial culture differs from the entrepreneurial culture that develops when leaders appear in organizations, managers and leaders are very different kinds of people. They differ in motivation, personal history, and in how they think and act.

Attitudes Toward Goals

Managers tend to adopt impersonal, if not passive, attitudes toward goals. Managerial goals arise out of necessities rather than desires and, therefore, are deeply embedded in their organization's history and culture.

Frederic G. Donner, chairman and chief executive officer of General Motors from 1958 to 1967, expressed this kind of attitude toward goals in defining GM's position on product development:

> *"To meet the challenge of the marketplace, we must recognize changes in customer needs and desires far enough ahead to have the right products in the right places at the right time and in the right quantity.*
>
> *"We must balance trends in preference against the many compromises that are necessary to make a final product that is both reliable and good looking, that performs well and that sells at a competitive price in the necessary volume. We must design not just the cars we would like to build but, more important, the cars that our customers want to buy."*[2]

Nowhere in this statement is there a notion that consumer tastes and preferences arise in part as a result of what manufacturers do. In reality, through product design, advertising, and promotion, consumers learn to like what they then say they need. Few would argue that people who enjoy taking snapshots need a camera that also develops pictures. But in response to a need for novelty, convenience, and a shorter interval between acting (snapping the picture) and gaining pleasure (seeing the shot), the Polaroid camera succeeded in the marketplace. It is inconceivable that Edwin Land responded to impressions of consumer need. Instead, he translated a technology (polarization of light) into a product, which proliferated and stimulated consumers' desires.

The example of Polaroid and Land suggests how leaders think about goals. They are active instead of reactive, shaping ideas instead of responding to them. Leaders adopt a personal and active attitude toward goals. The influence a leader exerts in altering moods, evoking images and expectations, and in establishing specific desires and objectives determines the direction a business takes. The net result of this influence changes the way people think about what is desirable, possible, and necessary.

Conceptions of Work

Managers tend to view work as an enabling process involving some combination of people and ideas interacting to establish strategies and make decisions. They help the process along by calculating the interests in opposition, planning when controversial issues should surface, and reducing tensions. In this enabling process, managers' tactics appear flexible: on one hand, they negotiate and bargain; on the other, they use rewards, punishments, and other forms of coercion.

Alfred P. Sloan's actions at General Motors illustrate how this process works in situations of conflict. The time was the early 1920s when Ford Motor Company still dominated the automobile industry using, as did General Motors, the conventional water-cooled engine. With the full backing of Pierre du Pont, Charles Kettering dedicated himself to the design of an air-cooled copper engine, which, if successful, would be a great technical and marketing coup for GM. Kettering believed in his product, but the manufacturing division heads opposed the new design on two grounds: first, it was technically unreliable, and second, the corporation was putting all its eggs in one basket by investing in a new product instead of attending to the current marketing situation.

In the summer of 1923, after a series of false starts and after its decision to recall the copper engine Chevrolets from dealers and customers, GM management scrapped the project. When it dawned on Kettering that the company had rejected the engine, he was deeply discouraged and wrote to Sloan that, without the "organized resistance" against the project, it would have succeeded and that, unless the project were saved, he would leave the company.

Alfred Sloan was all too aware that Kettering was unhappy and indeed intended to leave General Motors. Sloan was also aware that, while the manufacturing divisions strongly opposed the new engine, Pierre du Pont supported Kettering. Further, Sloan had himself gone on record in a letter to Kettering less than two years earlier expressing full confidence in him. The problem Sloan had was how to make his decision stick, keep Kettering in the organization (he was much too valuable to lose), avoid alienating du Pont, and encourage the division heads to continue developing product lines using conventional water-cooled engines.

Sloan's actions in the face of this conflict reveal much about how managers work. First, he tried to reassure

Kettering by presenting the problem in a very ambiguous fashion, suggesting that he and the executive committee sided with Kettering, but that it would not be practical to force the divisions to do what they were opposed to. He presented the problem as being a question of the people, not the product. Second, he proposed to reorganize around the problem by consolidating all functions in a new division that would be responsible for the design, production, and marketing of the new engine. This solution appeared as ambiguous as his efforts to placate Kettering. Sloan wrote:

> *"My plan was to create an independent pilot operation under the sole jurisdiction of Mr. Kettering, a kind of copper-cooled car division. Mr. Kettering would designate his own chief engineer and his production staff to solve the technical problems of manufacture."*[3]

Sloan did not discuss the practical value of this solution, which included saddling an inventor with management responsibility, but in effect, he used this plan to limit his conflict with Pierre du Pont.

Essentially, the managerial solution that Sloan arranged limited the options available to others. The structural solution narrowed choices, even limiting emotional reactions to the point where the key people could do nothing but go along. It allowed Sloan to say in his memorandum to du Pont, "We have discussed the matter with Mr. Kettering at some length this morning, and he agrees with us absolutely on every point we made. He appears to receive the suggestion enthusiastically and has every confidence that it can be put across along these lines."[4]

Sloan placated people who opposed his views by developing a structural solution that appeared to give something but in reality only limited options. He could then authorize the car division's general manager, with whom he basically agreed, to move quickly in designing water-cooled cars for the immediate market demand.

Years later, Sloan wrote, evidently with tongue in cheek, "The copper-cooled car never came up again in a big way. It just died out; I don't know why."[5]

To get people to accept solutions to problems, managers continually need to coordinate and balance opposing views. Interestingly enough, this type of work has much in common with what diplomats and mediators do, with Henry Kissinger apparently an outstanding practitioner. Managers aim to shift balances of power toward solutions acceptable as compromises among conflicting values.

Leaders work in the opposite direction. Where managers act to limit choices, leaders develop fresh approaches to long-standing problems and open issues to new options. To be effective, leaders must project their ideas onto images that excite people and only then develop choices that give those images substance.

John F. Kennedy's brief presidency shows both the strengths and weaknesses connected with the excitement leaders generate in their work. In his inaugural address he said, "Let every nation know, whether it wishes us well or ill, that we shall pay any price, bear any burden, meet any hardship, support any friend, oppose any foe, in order to assure the survival and the success of liberty."

This much-quoted statement forced people to react beyond immediate concerns and to identify with Kennedy and with important shared ideals. On closer scrutiny, however, the statement is absurd because it promises a position, which, if adopted, as in the Vietnam War, could produce disastrous results. Yet unless expectations are aroused and mobilized, with all the dangers of frustration inherent in heightened desire, new thinking and new choice can never come to light.

Leaders work from high-risk positions; indeed, they are often temperamentally disposed to seek out risk and danger, especially where the chance of opportunity and reward appears promising. From my observations, the reason one individual seeks risks while another approaches problems conservatively depends more on his or her personality and less on conscious choice. For those who become managers, a survival instinct dominates the need for risk, and with that instinct comes an ability to tolerate mundane, practical work. Leaders sometimes react to mundane work as to an affliction.

Relations with Others

Managers prefer to work with people; they avoid solitary activity because it makes them anxious. Several years ago, I directed studies on the psychological aspects of careers. The need to seek out others with whom to work and collaborate seemed to stand out as an important characteristic of managers. When asked, for example, to write imaginative stories in response to a picture showing a single figure (a boy contemplating a violin or a man silhouetted in a state of reflection), managers populated their stories with people. The following is an example of a manager's imaginative story about the young boy contemplating a violin:

> *Mom and Dad insisted that their son take music lessons so that someday he can become a concert musician. His instrument was ordered and had just arrived. The boy is weighing the alternatives of playing football with the*

*other kids or playing with the squeak box. He can't under-
stand how his parents could think a violin is better than a
touchdown.*

*After four months of practicing the violin, the boy has
had more than enough, Dad is going out of his mind, and
Mom is willing to give in reluctantly to their wishes. Football season is now over, but a good third baseman will
take the field next spring.*

This story illustrates two themes that clarify managerial attitudes toward human relations. The first, as I have
suggested, is to seek out activity with other people (that
is, the football team), and the second is to maintain a low
level of emotional involvement in those relationships.
Low emotional involvement appears in the writer's use
of conventional metaphors, even clichés, and in the
depiction of the ready transformation of potential conflict into harmonious decisions. In this case, the boy,
Mom, and Dad agree to give up the violin for sports.

These two themes may seem paradoxical, but their
coexistence supports what a manager does, including
reconciling differences, seeking compromises, and establishing a balance of power. The story further demon-
strates that managers may lack empathy, or the capacity
to sense intuitively the thoughts and feelings of others.
Consider another story written to the same stimulus picture by someone thought of as a leader by his peers:

*This little boy has the appearance of being a sincere
artist, one who is deeply affected by the violin, and has an
intense desire to master the instrument.*

*He seems to have just completed his normal practice
session and appears to be somewhat crestfallen at his
inability to produce the sounds that he is sure lie within
the violin.*

> *He appears to be in the process of making a vow to*
> *himself to expend the necessary time and effort to play*
> *this instrument until he satisfies himself that he is able to*
> *bring forth the qualities of music that he feels within*
> *himself.*
> *With this type of determination and carry-through,*
> *this boy became one of the great violinists of his day.*

Empathy is not simply a matter of paying attention to other people. It is also the capacity to take in emotional signals and make them meaningful in a relationship. People who describe another person as "deeply affected," with "intense desire," "crestfallen," and as one who can "vow to himself" would seem to have an inner perceptiveness that they can use in their relationships with others.

Managers relate to people according to the role they play in a sequence of events or in a decision-making process, while leaders, who are concerned with ideas, relate in more intuitive and empathetic ways. The distinction is simply between a manager's attention to *how* things get done and a leader's to *what* the events and decisions mean to participants.

In recent years, managers have adopted from game theory the notion that decision-making events can be one of two types: the win-lose situation (or zero-sum game) or the win-win situation in which everybody in the action comes out ahead. Managers strive to convert win-lose into win-win situations as part of the process of reconciling differences among people and maintaining balances of power.

As an illustration, take the decision of how to allocate capital resources among operating divisions in a large, decentralized organization. On the surface, the dollars available for distribution are limited at any given time. Presumably, therefore, the more one division gets, the less is available for other divisions.

Managers tend to view this situation (as it affects human relations) as a conversion issue: how to make what seems like a win-lose problem into a win-win problem. From that perspective, several solutions come to mind. First, the manager focuses others' attention on procedure and not on substance. Here the players become engrossed in the bigger problem of *how* to make decisions, not *what* decisions to make. Once committed to the bigger problem, these people have to support the outcome since they were involved in formulating the decision-making rules. Because they believe in the rules they formulated, they will accept present losses, believing that next time they will win.

Second, the manager communicates to subordinates indirectly, using "signals" instead of "messages." A signal holds a number of implicit positions, while a message clearly states a position. Signals are inconclusive and subject to reinterpretation should people become upset and angry; messages involve the direct consequence that some people will indeed not like what they hear. The nature of messages heightens emotional response and makes managers anxious. With signals, the question of who wins and who loses often becomes obscured.

Third, the manager plays for time. Managers seem to recognize that with the passage of time and the delay of major decisions, compromises emerge that take the sting out of win-lose situations, and the original "game" will be superseded by additional situations. Compromises mean that one may win and lose simultaneously, depending on which of the games one evaluates.

There are undoubtedly many other tactical moves managers use to change human situations from win-lose to win-win. But the point is that such tactics focus on the decision-making process itself, and that process interests managers rather than leaders. Tactical interests involve costs as well as benefits; they make organizations fatter in bureaucratic and political intrigue and leaner in direct, hard activity and warm human relationships. Consequently, one often hears subordinates characterize managers as inscrutable, detached, and manipulative. These adjectives arise from the subordinates' perception that they are linked together in a process whose purpose is to maintain a controlled as well as rational and equitable structure.

In contrast, one often hears leaders referred to with adjectives rich in emotional content. Leaders attract strong feelings of identity and difference or of love and hate. Human relations in leader-dominated structures often appear turbulent, intense, and at times even disorganized. Such an atmosphere intensifies individual motivation and often produces unanticipated outcomes.

Senses of Self

In *The Varieties of Religious Experience*, William James describes two basic personality types, "once-born" and "twice-born." People of the former personality type are those for whom adjustments to life have been straightforward and whose lives have been more or less a peaceful flow since birth. Twice-borns, on the other hand, have not had an easy time of it. Their lives are marked by a continual struggle to attain some sense of order. Unlike onceborns, they cannot take things for granted. According to

James, these personalities have equally different world-views. For a once-born personality, the sense of self as a guide to conduct and attitude derives from a feeling of being at home and in harmony with one's environment. For a twice-born, the sense of self derives from a feeling of profound separateness.

A sense of belonging or of being separate has a practical significance for the kinds of investments managers and leaders make in their careers. Managers see themselves as conservators and regulators of an existing order of affairs with which they personally identify and from which they gain rewards. A manager's sense of self-worth is enhanced by perpetuating and strengthening existing institutions: he or she is performing in a role that harmonizes with ideals of duty and responsibility. William James had this harmony in mind—this sense of self as flowing easily to and from the outer world—in defining a once-born personality.

Leaders tend to be twice-born personalities, people who feel separate from their environment. They may work in organizations, but they never belong to them. Their sense of who they are does not depend on memberships, work roles, or other social indicators of identity. And that perception of identity may form the theoretical basis for explaining why certain individuals seek opportunities for change. The methods to bring about change may be technological, political, or ideological, but the object is the same: to profoundly alter human, economic, and political relationships.

In considering the development of leadership, we have to examine two different courses of life history: (1) development through socialization, which prepares the individual to guide institutions and to maintain the existing balance of social relations; and (2) development through personal mastery, which impels an individual to struggle for psychological and social change. Society produces its managerial talent through the first line of development; leaders emerge through the second.

Development of Leadership

Every person's development begins with family. Each person experiences the traumas associated with separating from his or her parents, as well as the pain that follows such a wrench. In the same vein, all individuals face the difficulties of achieving self-regulation and self-control. But for some, perhaps a majority, the fortunes of childhood provide adequate gratifications and sufficient opportunities to find substitutes for rewards no longer available. Such individuals, the "once-borns," make moderate identifications with parents and find a harmony between what they expect and what they are able to realize from life.

But suppose the pains of separation are amplified by a combination of parental demands and individual needs to the degree that a sense of isolation, of being special, or of wariness disrupts the bonds that attach children to parents and other authority figures? Given a special aptitude under such conditions, the person becomes deeply involved in his or her inner world at the expense of interest in the outer world. For such a person, self-esteem no longer depends solely on positive attachments and real rewards. A form of self-reliance takes hold along with expectations of performance and achievement, and perhaps even the desire to do great works.

Such self-perceptions can come to nothing if the individual's talents are negligible. Even with strong talents, there are no guarantees that achievement will follow, let alone that the end result will be for good rather than evil. Other factors enter into development as well. For one, leaders are like artists and other gifted people who often struggle with neuroses; their ability to function varies considerably even over the short run, and some potential leaders lose the struggle altogether. Also, beyond early childhood, the development patterns that affect managers and leaders involve the selective influence of particular people. Managerial personalities form moderate and widely distributed attachments. Leaders, on the other hand, establish, and also break off, intensive one-to-one relationships.

It is a common observation that people with great talents are often indifferent students. No one, for example, could have predicted Einstein's great achievements on the basis of his mediocre record in school. The reason for mediocrity is obviously not the absence of ability. It may result, instead, from self-absorption and the inability to pay attention to the ordinary tasks at hand. The only sure way an individual can interrupt reverie-like preoccupation and self-absorption is to form a deep attachment to a great teacher or other person who understands and has the ability to communicate with the gifted individual.

Whether gifted individuals find what they need in one-to-one relationships depends on the availability of teachers, possibly parental surrogates, whose strengths lie in cultivating talent. Fortunately, when generations meet and the self-selections occur, we learn more about how to develop leaders and how talented people of different generations influence each other.

While apparently destined for mediocre careers, people who form important one-to-one apprenticeship relationships often are able to accelerate and intensify their development. The psychological readiness of an individual to benefit from such a relationship depends on some experience in life that forces that person to turn inward.

Consider Dwight Eisenhower, whose early career in the army foreshadowed very little about his future development. During World War I, while some of his West Point classmates were already experiencing the war firsthand in France, Eisenhower felt "embedded in the monotony and unsought safety of the Zone of the Interior . . . that was intolerable punishment."[6]

Shortly after World War I, Eisenhower, then a young officer somewhat pessimistic about his career chances, asked for a transfer to Panama to work under General Fox Connor, a senior officer whom he admired. The army turned down his request. This setback was very much on Eisenhower's mind when Ikey, his first born son, succumbed to influenza. Through some sense of responsibility for its own, the army then transferred Eisenhower to Panama, where he took up his duties under General Connor with the shadow of his lost son very much upon him.

In a relationship with the kind of father he would have wanted to be, Eisenhower reverted to being the son he had lost. And in this highly charged situation, he began to learn from his teacher. General Connor offered, and Eisenhower gladly took, a magnificent tutorial on the military. The effects of this relationship on Eisenhower cannot be measured quantitatively, but in examining his career path from that point, one cannot overestimate its significance.

As Eisenhower wrote later about Connor, "Life with General Connor was a sort of graduate school in military affairs and the humanities, leavened by a man who was experienced in his knowledge of men and their conduct. I can never adequately express my gratitude to this one gentleman. . . . In a lifetime of association with great

and good men, he is the one more or less invisible figure
to whom I owe an incalculable debt."[7]

Some time after his tour of duty with General Connor,
Eisenhower's breakthrough occurred. He received orders
to attend the Command and General Staff School at Fort
Leavenworth, one of the most competitive schools in the
army. It was a coveted appointment, and Eisenhower
took advantage of the opportunity. Unlike his performance in high school and West Point, his work at the
Command School was excellent; he was graduated first
in his class.

Psychological biographies of gifted people repeatedly
demonstrate the important part a teacher plays in developing an individual. Andrew Carnegie owed much to his
senior, Thomas A. Scott. As head of the Western Division
of the Pennsylvania Railroad, Scott recognized talent and
the desire to learn in the young telegrapher assigned to
him. By giving Carnegie increasing responsibility and by
providing him with the opportunity to learn through
close personal observation, Scott added to Carnegie's
self-confidence and sense of achievement. Because of his
own personal strength and achievement, Scott did not
fear Carnegie's aggressiveness. Rather, he gave it full play
in encouraging Carnegie's initiative.

Great teachers take risks. They bet initially on talent
they perceive in younger people. And they risk emotional
involvement in working closely with their juniors. The
risks do not always pay off, but the willingness to take
them appears to be crucial in developing leaders.

Can Organizations Develop Leaders?

A myth about how people learn and develop that seems
to have taken hold in American culture also dominates
thinking in business. The myth is that people learn best

from their peers. Supposedly, the threat of evaluation and even humiliation recedes in peer relations because of the tendency for mutual identification and the social restraints on authoritarian behavior among equals. Peer training in organizations occurs in various forms. The use, for example, of task forces made up of peers from several interested occupational groups (sales, production, research, and finance) supposedly removes the restraints of authority on the individual's willingness to assert and exchange ideas. As a result, so the theory goes, people interact more freely, listen more objectively to criticism and other points of view, and, finally, learn from this healthy interchange.

Another application of peer training exists in some large corporations, such as Philips N.V. in Holland, where organizational structure is built on the principle of joint responsibility of two peers, one representing the commercial end of the business and the other the technical. Formally, both hold equal responsibility for geographic operations or product groups, as the case may be. As a practical matter, it may turn out that one or the other of the peers dominates the management. Nevertheless, the main interaction is between two or more equals.

The principal question I raise about such arrangements is whether they perpetuate the managerial orientation and preclude the formation of one-to-one relationships between senior people and potential leaders.

Aware of the possible stifling effects of peer relationships on aggressiveness and individual initiative, another company, much smaller than Philips, utilizes joint responsibility of peers for operating units, with one important difference. The chief executive of this company encourages competition and rivalry among peers, ultimately rewarding the one who comes out on top with increased responsibility. These hybrid arrangements produce some unintended consequences that can be disastrous. There is no easy way to limit rivalry. Instead, it permeates all levels of the operation and opens the way for the formation of cliques in an atmosphere of intrigue.

One large, integrated oil company has accepted the importance of developing leaders through the direct influence of senior on junior executives. The chairman and chief executive officer regularly selects one talented university graduate whom he appoints his special assistant, and with whom he will work closely for a year. At the end of the year, the junior executive becomes available for assignment to one of the operating divisions, where he or she will be assigned to a responsible post rather than a training position. This apprenticeship acquaints the junior executive firsthand with the use of power and with the important antidotes to the power disease called *hubris*—performance and integrity.

Working in one-to-one relationships, where there is a formal and recognized difference in the power of the players, takes a great deal of tolerance for emotional interchange. This interchange, inevitable in close working arrangements, probably accounts for the reluctance of many executives to become involved in such relationships. *Fortune* carried an interesting story on the departure of a key executive, John W. Hanley, from the top management of Procter & Gamble to the chief executive officer position at Monsanto.[8] According to this account, the chief executive and chairman of P&G passed over Hanley for appointment to the presidency, instead naming another executive vice president to this post.

The chairman evidently felt he could not work well with Hanley who, by his own acknowledgment, was aggressive, eager to experiment and change practices, and constantly challenged his superior. A chief executive officer naturally has the right to select people with whom he feels congenial. But I wonder whether a greater capacity on the part of senior officers to tolerate the competitive impulses and behavior of their subordinates might not be healthy for corporations. At least a greater tolerance for interchange would not favor the managerial team player at the expense of the individual who might become a leader.

I am constantly surprised at the frequency with which chief executives feel threatened by open challenges to their ideas, as though the source of their authority, rather than their specific ideas, was at issue. In one case, a chief executive officer, who was troubled by the aggressiveness and sometimes outright rudeness of one of his talented vice presidents, used various indirect methods such as group meetings and hints from outside directors to avoid dealing with his subordinate. I advised the executive to deal head-on with what irritated him. I suggested that by direct, face-to-face confrontation, both he and his subordinate would learn to validate the distinction between the authority to be preserved and the issues to be debated.

The ability to confront is also the ability to tolerate aggressive interchange. And that skill not only has the net effect of stripping away the veils of ambiguity and signaling so characteristic of managerial cultures, but also it encourages the emotional relationships leaders need if they are to survive.

Notes

1. John D. Rockefeller III, *The Second American Revolution* (HarperCollins, 1973).

2. Alfred P. Sloan, Jr., *My Years with General Motors* (New York: Doubleday, 1964).

3. Ibid.

4. Ibid.

5. Ibid.

6. Dwight D. Eisenhower, *At Ease: Stories I Tell to Friends* (New York: Doubleday, 1967).

7. Ibid.

8. "Jack Hanley Got There by Selling Harder," *Fortune*, November 1976.

Originally published in May–June 1977
Reprint R0401G

What Makes a Leader?

DANIEL GOLEMAN

Executive Summary

WHEN ASKED TO DEFINE the ideal leader, many
would emphasize traits such as intelligence, toughness,
determination, and vision—the qualities traditionally associated with leadership. Such skills and smarts are necessary but insufficient qualities for the leader. Often left off
the list are softer, more personal qualities—but they are
also essential. Although a certain degree of analytical
and technical skill is a minimum requirement for success,
studies indicate that emotional intelligence may be the
key attribute that distinguishes outstanding performers
from those who are merely adequate.

Psychologist and author Daniel Goleman first brought
the term "emotional intelligence" to a wide audience
with his 1995 book of the same name, and Goleman
first applied the concept to business with this 1998 classic HBR article. In his research at nearly 200 large,

global companies, Goleman found that truly effective leaders are distinguished by a high degree of emotional intelligence. Without it, a person can have first-class training, an incisive mind, and an endless supply of good ideas, but he still won't be a great leader.

The chief components of emotional intelligence—self-awareness, self-regulation, motivation, empathy, and social skill—can sound unbusinesslike, but Goleman, co-chair of the Consortium for Research on Emotional Intelligence in Organizations, based at Rutgers University, found direct ties between emotional intelligence and measurable business results. The notion of emotional intelligence and its relevance to business has continued to spark debate over the past six years, but Goleman's article remains the definitive reference on the subject, with a detailed discussion of each component of emotional intelligence, how to recognize it in potential leaders, how and why it connects to performance, and how it can be learned.

It was Daniel Goleman who first brought the term "emotional intelligence" to a wide audience with his 1995 book of that name, and it was Goleman who first applied the concept to business with his 1998 HBR article, reprinted here. In his research at nearly 200 large, global companies, Goleman found that while the qualities traditionally associated with leadership—such as intelligence, toughness, determination, and vision—are required for success, they are insufficient. Truly effective leaders are also distinguished by a high degree of emotional intelligence, which includes self-awareness, self-regulation, motivation, empathy, and social skill.

These qualities may sound "soft" and unbusinesslike, but Goleman found direct ties between emotional intelligence and measurable business results. While emotional intelligence's relevance to business has continued to spark debate over the past six years, Goleman's article remains the definitive reference on the subject, with a description of each component of emotional intelligence and a detailed discussion of how to recognize it in potential leaders, how and why it connects to performance, and how it can be learned.

Every businessperson knows a story about a highly intelligent, highly skilled executive who was promoted into a leadership position only to fail at the job. And they also know a story about someone with solid— but not extraordinary—intellectual abilities and technical skills who was promoted into a similar position and then soared.

Such anecdotes support the widespread belief that identifying individuals with the "right stuff" to be leaders is more art than science. After all, the personal styles of superb leaders vary: Some leaders are subdued and analytical; others shout their manifestos from the mountaintops. And just as important, different situations call for different types of leadership. Most mergers need a sensitive negotiator at the helm, whereas many turnarounds require a more forceful authority.

I have found, however, that the most effective leaders are alike in one crucial way: They all have a high degree of what has come to be known as *emotional intelligence*. It's not that IQ and technical skills are irrelevant. They do matter, but mainly as "threshold capabilities"; that is, they are the entry-level requirements for executive positions. But my research, along with other recent studies, clearly shows that emotional intelligence is the sine qua non of leadership. Without it, a person can have the best training in the world, an incisive, analytical mind, and an endless supply of smart ideas, but he still won't make a great leader.

In the course of the past year, my colleagues and I have focused on how emotional intelligence operates at work. We have examined the relationship between emotional intelligence and effective performance, especially in leaders. And we have observed how emotional intelligence shows itself on the job. How can you tell if someone has high emotional intelligence, for example, and how can you recognize it in yourself? In the following pages, we'll explore these questions, taking each of the components of emotional intelligence—self-awareness, self-regulation, motivation, empathy, and social skill—in turn. See the exhibit "The Five Components of Emotional Intelligence at Work" for an overview.

Evaluating Emotional Intelligence

Most large companies today have employed trained psychologists to develop what are known as "competency models" to aid them in identifying, training, and promoting likely stars in the leadership firmament. The psychologists have also developed such models for lower-level positions. And in recent years, I have analyzed competency models from 188 companies, most of which were large and global and included the likes of Lucent Technologies, British Airways, and Credit Suisse.

In carrying out this work, my objective was to determine which personal capabilities drove outstanding performance within these organizations, and to what degree

The Five Components of Emotional Intelligence at Work

	Definition	Hallmarks
Self-Awareness	the ability to recognize and understand your moods, emotions, and drives, as well as their effect on others	self-confidence realistic self-assessment self-deprecating sense of humor
Self-Regulation	the ability to control or redirect disruptive impulses and moods the propensity to suspend judgment—to think before acting	trustworthiness and integrity comfort with ambiguity openness to change
Motivation	a passion to work for reasons that go beyond money or status a propensity to pursue goals with energy and persistence	strong drive to achieve optimism, even in the face of failure organizational commitment
Empathy	the ability to understand the emotional makeup of other people skill in treating people according to their emotional reactions	expertise in building and retaining talent cross-cultural sensitivity service to clients and customers
Social Skill	proficiency in managing relationships and building networks an ability to find common ground and build rapport	effectiveness in leading change persuasiveness expertise in building and leading teams

they did so. I grouped capabilities into three categories:
purely technical skills like accounting and business planning; cognitive abilities like analytical reasoning; and
competencies demonstrating emotional intelligence,
such as the ability to work with others and effectiveness
in leading change.

To create some of the competency models, psychologists asked senior managers at the companies to identify
the capabilities that typified the organization's most outstanding leaders. To create other models, the psychologists used objective criteria, such as a division's profitability, to differentiate the star performers at senior
levels within their organizations from the average ones.
Those individuals were then extensively interviewed and
tested, and their capabilities were compared. This process resulted in the creation of lists of ingredients for
highly effective leaders. The lists ranged in length from
seven to 15 items and included such ingredients as initiative and strategic vision.

When I analyzed all this data, I found dramatic
results. To be sure, intellect was a driver of outstanding
performance. Cognitive skills such as big-picture thinking and long-term vision were particularly important.
But when I calculated the ratio of technical skills, IQ, and
emotional intelligence as ingredients of excellent performance, emotional intelligence proved to be twice as
important as the others for jobs at all levels.

Moreover, my analysis showed that emotional intelligence played an increasingly important role at the highest levels of the company, where differences in technical
skills are of negligible importance. In other words, the
higher the rank of a person considered to be a star per-
former, the more emotional intelligence capabilities
showed up as the reason for his or her effectiveness.

When I compared star performers with average ones in senior leadership positions, nearly 90% of the difference in their profiles was attributable to emotional intelligence factors rather than cognitive abilities.

Other researchers have confirmed that emotional intelligence not only distinguishes outstanding leaders but can also be linked to strong performance. The findings of the late David McClelland, the renowned researcher in human and organizational behavior, are a good example. In a 1996 study of a global food and beverage company, McClelland found that when senior managers had a critical mass of emotional intelligence capabilities, their divisions outperformed yearly earnings goals by 20%. Meanwhile, division leaders without that critical mass underperformed by almost the same amount. McClelland's findings, interestingly, held as true in the company's U.S. divisions as in its divisions in Asia and Europe.

In short, the numbers are beginning to tell us a persuasive story about the link between a company's success and the emotional intelligence of its leaders. And just as important, research is also demonstrating that people can, if they take the right approach, develop their emotional intelligence. (See "Can Emotional Intelligence Be Learned?" at the end of this article.)

Self-Awareness

Self-awareness is the first component of emotional intelligence—which makes sense when one considers that the Delphic oracle gave the advice to "know thyself" thousands of years ago. Self-awareness means having a deep understanding of one's emotions, strengths, weaknesses, needs, and drives. People with strong self-awareness are neither overly critical nor unrealistically hopeful. Rather, they are honest—with themselves and with others.

People who have a high degree of self-awareness recognize how their feelings affect them, other people, and their job performance. Thus, a self-aware person who knows that tight deadlines bring out the worst in him plans his time carefully and gets his work done well in advance. Another person with high self-awareness will be able to work with a demanding client. She will understand the client's impact on her moods and the deeper reasons for her frustration. "Their trivial demands take us away from the real work that needs to be done," she might explain. And she will go one step further and turn her anger into something constructive.

Self-awareness extends to a person's understanding of his or her values and goals. Someone who is highly self-aware knows where he is headed and why; so, for example, he will be able to be firm in turning down a job offer that is tempting financially but does not fit with his principles or long-term goals. A person who lacks self-awareness is apt to make decisions that bring on inner turmoil by treading on buried values. "The money looked good so I signed on," someone might say two years into a job, "but the work means so little to me that I'm constantly bored." The decisions of self-aware people mesh with their values; consequently, they often find work to be energizing.

How can one recognize self-awareness? First and foremost, it shows itself as candor and an ability to assess oneself realistically. People with high self-awareness are able to speak accurately and openly—although not necessarily effusively or confessionally—about their emotions and the impact they have on their work. For instance, one manager I know of was skeptical about a new personal-shopper service that her company, a major department-store chain, was about to introduce. Without prompting from her team or her boss, she offered them an explanation: "It's hard for me to get behind the rollout of this service," she admitted, "because I really wanted to run the project, but I wasn't selected. Bear with me while I deal with that." The manager did indeed examine her feelings; a week later, she was supporting the project fully.

Such self-knowledge often shows itself in the hiring process. Ask a candidate to describe a time he got carried away by his feelings and did something he later regretted. Self-aware candidates will be frank in admitting to failure—and will often tell their tales with a smile. One of the hallmarks of self-awareness is a self-deprecating sense of humor.

Self-awareness can also be identified during performance reviews. Self-aware people know—and are comfortable talking about—their limitations and strengths, and they often demonstrate a thirst for constructive criticism. By contrast, people with low self-awareness interpret the message that they need to improve as a threat or a sign of failure.

Self-aware people can also be recognized by their self-confidence. They have a firm grasp of their capabilities and are less likely to set themselves up to fail by, for example, overstretching on assignments. They know, too, when to ask for help. And the risks they take on the job are calculated. They won't ask for a challenge that they know they can't handle alone. They'll play to their strengths.

Consider the actions of a midlevel employee who was invited to sit in on a strategy meeting with her company's top executives. Although she was the most junior person in the room, she did not sit there quietly, listening in awestruck or fearful silence. She knew she had a head for clear logic and the skill to present ideas persuasively, and she offered cogent suggestions about the company's strategy. At the same time, her self-awareness stopped her from wandering into territory where she knew she was weak.

Despite the value of having self-aware people in the workplace, my research indicates that senior executives don't often give self-awareness the credit it deserves when they look for potential leaders. Many executives mistake candor about feelings for "wimpiness" and fail to give due respect to employees who openly acknowledge their shortcomings. Such people are too readily dismissed as "not tough enough" to lead others.

In fact, the opposite is true. In the first place, people generally admire and respect candor. Furthermore, leaders are constantly required to make judgment calls that require a candid assessment of capabilities—their own and those of others. Do we have the management expertise to acquire a competitor? Can we launch a new product within six months? People who assess themselves honestly—that is, self-aware people—are well suited to do the same for the organizations they run.

Self-Regulation

Biological impulses drive our emotions. We cannot do away with them—but we can do much to manage them. Self-regulation, which is like an ongoing inner conversation, is the component of emotional intelligence that frees us from being prisoners of our feelings. People engaged in such a conversation feel bad moods and emotional impulses just as everyone else does, but they find ways to control them and even to channel them in useful ways.

Imagine an executive who has just watched a team of his employees present a botched analysis to the company's board of directors. In the gloom that follows, the executive might find himself tempted to pound on the table in anger or kick over a chair. He could leap up and scream at the group. Or he might maintain a grim silence, glaring at everyone before stalking off.

But if he had a gift for self-regulation, he would choose a different approach. He would pick his words carefully, acknowledging the team's poor performance without rushing to any hasty judgment. He would then step back to consider the reasons for the failure. Are they personal—a lack of effort? Are there any mitigating factors? What was his role in the debacle? After considering these questions, he would call the team together, lay out the incident's consequences, and offer his feelings about it. He would then present his analysis of the problem and a well-considered solution.

Why does self-regulation matter so much for leaders? First of all, people who are in control of their feelings and impulses—that is, people who are reasonable—are able to create an environment of trust and fairness. In such an environment, politics and infighting are sharply reduced and productivity is high. Talented people flock to the organization and aren't tempted to leave. And self-regulation has a trickle-down effect. No one wants to be known as a hothead when the boss is known for her calm approach. Fewer bad moods at the top mean fewer throughout the organization.

Second, self-regulation is important for competitive reasons. Everyone knows that business today is rife with ambiguity and change. Companies merge and break apart regularly. Technology transforms work at a dizzying pace. People who have mastered their emotions are able to roll with the changes. When a new program is announced, they don't panic; instead, they are able to suspend judgment, seek out information, and listen to the executives as they explain the new program. As the initiative moves forward, these people are able to move with it.

Sometimes they even lead the way. Consider the case of a manager at a large manufacturing company. Like her colleagues, she had used a certain software program for five years. The program drove how she collected and reported data and how she thought about the company's strategy. One day, senior executives announced that a new program was to be installed that would radically change how information was gathered and assessed within the organization. While many people in the company complained bitterly about how disruptive the change would be, the manager mulled over the reasons for the new program and was convinced of its potential to improve performance. She eagerly attended training sessions—some of her colleagues refused to do so—and was eventually promoted to run several divisions, in part because she used the new technology so effectively.

I want to push the importance of self-regulation to leadership even further and make the case that it enhances integrity, which is not only a personal virtue but also an organizational strength. Many of the bad things that happen in companies are a function of impulsive behavior. People rarely plan to exaggerate profits, pad expense accounts, dip into the till, or abuse power for selfish ends. Instead, an opportunity presents itself, and people with low impulse control just say yes.

By contrast, consider the behavior of the senior executive at a large food company. The executive was scrupulously honest in his negotiations with local distributors. He would routinely lay out his cost structure in detail, thereby giving the distributors a realistic understanding of the company's pricing. This approach meant the executive couldn't always drive a hard bargain. Now, on occasion, he felt the urge to increase profits by withholding information about the company's costs. But he challenged that impulse—he saw that it made more sense in the long run to counteract it. His emotional self-regulation paid off in strong, lasting relationships with distributors that benefited the company more than any short-term financial gains would have.

The signs of emotional self-regulation, therefore, are easy to see: a propensity for reflection and thoughtfulness; comfort with ambiguity and change; and integrity—an ability to say no to impulsive urges.

Like self-awareness, self-regulation often does not get its due. People who can master their emotions are sometimes seen as cold fish—their considered responses are taken as a lack of passion. People with fiery temperaments are frequently thought of as "classic" leaders— their outbursts are considered hallmarks of charisma and power. But when such people make it to the top, their impulsiveness often works against them. In my research, extreme displays of negative emotion have never emerged as a driver of good leadership.

Motivation

If there is one trait that virtually all effective leaders have, it is motivation. They are driven to achieve beyond expectations—their own and everyone else's. The key word here is *achieve*. Plenty of people are motivated by external factors, such as a big salary or the status that comes from having an impressive title or being part of a prestigious company. By contrast, those with leadership potential are motivated by a deeply embedded desire to achieve for the sake of achievement.

If you are looking for leaders, how can you identify people who are motivated by the drive to achieve rather than by external rewards? The first sign is a passion for the work itself—such people seek out creative challenges, love to learn, and take great pride in a job well done. They also display an unflagging energy to do things better. People with such energy often seem restless with the status quo. They are persistent with their questions about why things are done one way rather than another; they are eager to explore new approaches to their work.

A cosmetics company manager, for example, was frustrated that he had to wait two weeks to get sales results from people in the field. He finally tracked down an automated phone system that would beep each of his salespeople at 5 pm every day. An automated message then prompted them to punch in their numbers—how many calls and sales they had made that day. The system shortened the feedback time on sales results from weeks to hours.

That story illustrates two other common traits of people who are driven to achieve. They are forever raising the performance bar, and they like to keep score. Take the performance bar first. During performance reviews, people with high levels of motivation might ask to be "stretched" by their superiors. Of course, an employee who combines self-awareness with internal motivation will recognize her limits—but she won't settle for objectives that seem too easy to fulfill.

And it follows naturally that people who are driven to do better also want a way of tracking progress—their own, their team's, and their company's. Whereas people with low achievement motivation are often fuzzy about results, those with high achievement motivation often keep score by tracking such hard measures as profitability or market share. I know of a money manager who starts and ends his day on the Internet, gauging the performance of his stock fund against four industry-set benchmarks.

Interestingly, people with high motivation remain optimistic even when the score is against them. In such cases, self-regulation combines with achievement motivation to overcome the frustration and depression that come after a setback or failure. Take the case of an another portfolio manager at a large investment company. After several successful years, her fund tumbled for three consecutive quarters, leading three large institutional clients to shift their business elsewhere.

Some executives would have blamed the nosedive on circumstances outside their control; others might have seen the setback as evidence of personal failure. This portfolio manager, however, saw an opportunity to prove she could lead a turnaround. Two years later, when she was promoted to a very senior level in the company, she described the experience as "the best thing that ever happened to me; I learned so much from it."

Executives trying to recognize high levels of achievement motivation in their people can look for one last piece of evidence: commitment to the organization. When people love their jobs for the work itself, they often feel committed to the organizations that make that work possible. Committed employees are likely to stay with an organization even when they are pursued by headhunters waving money.

It's not difficult to understand how and why a motivation to achieve translates into strong leadership. If you

set the performance bar high for yourself, you will do the
same for the organization when you are in a position to
do so. Likewise, a drive to surpass goals and an interest
in keeping score can be contagious. Leaders with these
traits can often build a team of managers around them
with the same traits. And of course, optimism and organizational commitment are fundamental to leadership—
just try to imagine running a company without them.

Empathy

Of all the dimensions of emotional intelligence, empathy
is the most easily recognized. We have all felt the empathy of a sensitive teacher or friend; we have all been
struck by its absence in an unfeeling coach or boss. But
when it comes to business, we rarely hear people praised,
let alone rewarded, for their empathy. The very word
seems unbusinesslike, out of place amid the tough realities of the marketplace.

But empathy doesn't mean a kind of "I'm OK, you're
OK" mushiness. For a leader, that is, it doesn't mean
adopting other people's emotions as one's own and trying to please everybody. That would be a nightmare—it
would make action impossible. Rather, empathy means
thoughtfully considering employees' feelings—along
with other factors—in the process of making intelligent
decisions.

For an example of empathy in action, consider what
happened when two giant brokerage companies merged,
creating redundant jobs in all their divisions. One division
manager called his people together and gave a gloomy
speech that emphasized the number of people who would
soon be fired. The manager of another division gave his
people a different kind of speech. He was up-front about

his own worry and confusion, and he promised to keep people informed and to treat everyone fairly.

The difference between these two managers was empathy. The first manager was too worried about his own fate to consider the feelings of his anxiety-stricken colleagues. The second knew intuitively what his people were feeling, and he acknowledged their fears with his words. Is it any surprise that the first manager saw his division sink as many demoralized people, especially the most talented, departed? By contrast, the second manager continued to be a strong leader, his best people stayed, and his division remained as productive as ever.

Empathy is particularly important today as a component of leadership for at least three reasons: the increasing use of teams; the rapid pace of globalization; and the growing need to retain talent.

Consider the challenge of leading a team. As anyone who has ever been a part of one can attest, teams are cauldrons of bubbling emotions. They are often charged with reaching a consensus—which is hard enough with two people and much more difficult as the numbers increase. Even in groups with as few as four or five members, alliances form and clashing agendas get set. A team's leader must be able to sense and understand the viewpoints of everyone around the table.

That's exactly what a marketing manager at a large information technology company was able to do when she was appointed to lead a troubled team. The group was in turmoil, overloaded by work and missing deadlines. Tensions were high among the members. Tinkering with procedures was not enough to bring the group together and make it an effective part of the company.

So the manager took several steps. In a series of one-on-one sessions, she took the time to listen to everyone in the group—what was frustrating them, how they rated their colleagues, whether they felt they had been ignored. And then she directed the team in a way that brought it together: She encouraged people to speak more openly about their frustrations, and she helped people raise constructive complaints during meetings. In short, her empathy allowed her to understand her team's emotional makeup. The result was not just heightened collaboration among members but also added business, as the team was called on for help by a wider range of internal clients.

Globalization is another reason for the rising importance of empathy for business leaders. Cross-cultural dialogue can easily lead to miscues and misunderstandings. Empathy is an antidote. People who have it are attuned to subtleties in body language; they can hear the message beneath the words being spoken. Beyond that, they have a deep understanding of both the existence and the importance of cultural and ethnic differences.

Consider the case of an American consultant whose team had just pitched a project to a potential Japanese client. In its dealings with Americans, the team was accustomed to being bombarded with questions after such a proposal, but this time it was greeted with a long silence. Other members of the team, taking the silence as disapproval, were ready to pack and leave. The lead consultant gestured them to stop. Although he was not particularly familiar with Japanese culture, he read the client's face and posture and sensed not rejection but interest—even deep consideration. He was right: When the client finally spoke, it was to give the consulting firm the job.

Finally, empathy plays a key role in the retention of talent, particularly in today's information economy.

Leaders have always needed empathy to develop and keep good people, but today the stakes are higher. When good people leave, they take the company's knowledge with them.

That's where coaching and mentoring come in. It has repeatedly been shown that coaching and mentoring pay off not just in better performance but also in increased job satisfaction and decreased turnover. But what makes coaching and mentoring work best is the nature of the relationship. Outstanding coaches and mentors get inside the heads of the people they are helping. They sense how to give effective feedback. They know when to push for better performance and when to hold back. In the way they motivate their protégés, they demonstrate empathy in action.

In what is probably sounding like a refrain, let me repeat that empathy doesn't get much respect in business. People wonder how leaders can make hard decisions if they are "feeling" for all the people who will be affected. But leaders with empathy do more than sympathize with people around them: They use their knowledge to improve their companies in subtle but important ways.

Social Skill

The first three components of emotional intelligence are self-management skills. The last two, empathy and social skill, concern a person's ability to manage relationships with others. As a component of emotional intelligence, social skill is not as simple as it sounds. It's not just a matter of friendliness, although people with high levels of social skill are rarely mean-spirited. Social skill, rather, is friendliness with a purpose: moving people in the direction you desire, whether that's agreement on a new marketing strategy or enthusiasm about a new product.

Socially skilled people tend to have a wide circle of acquaintances, and they have a knack for finding common ground with people of all kinds—a knack for building rapport. That doesn't mean they socialize continually; it means they work according to the assumption that nothing important gets done alone. Such people have a network in place when the time for action comes.

Social skill is the culmination of the other dimensions of emotional intelligence. People tend to be very effective at managing relationships when they can understand and control their own emotions and can empathize with the feelings of others. Even motivation contributes to social skill. Remember that people who are driven to achieve tend to be optimistic, even in the face of setbacks or failure. When people are upbeat, their "glow" is cast upon conversations and other social encounters. They are popular, and for good reason.

Because it is the outcome of the other dimensions of emotional intelligence, social skill is recognizable on the job in many ways that will by now sound familiar. Socially skilled people, for instance, are adept at managing teams—that's their empathy at work. Likewise, they are expert persuaders—a manifestation of self-awareness, self-regulation, and empathy combined. Given those skills, good persuaders know when to make an emotional plea, for instance, and when an appeal to reason will work better. And motivation, when publicly visible, makes such people excellent collaborators; their passion for the work spreads to others, and they are driven to find solutions.

But sometimes social skill shows itself in ways the other emotional intelligence components do not. For instance, socially skilled people may at times appear not to be working while at work. They seem to be idly schmoozing—chatting in the hallways with colleagues or joking around with people who are not even connected to their "real" jobs. Socially skilled people, however, don't think it makes sense to arbitrarily limit the scope of their relationships. They build bonds widely because they know that in these fluid times, they may need help someday from people they are just getting to know today.

For example, consider the case of an executive in the strategy department of a global computer manufacturer. By 1993, he was convinced that the company's future lay with the Internet. Over the course of the next year, he found kindred spirits and used his social skill to stitch together a virtual community that cut across levels, divisions, and nations. He then used this de facto team to put up a corporate Web site, among the first by a major company. And, on his own initiative, with no budget or formal status, he signed up the company to participate in an annual Internet industry convention. Calling on his allies and persuading various divisions to donate funds, he recruited more than 50 people from a dozen different units to represent the company at the convention.

Management took notice: Within a year of the conference, the executive's team formed the basis for the company's first Internet division, and he was formally put in charge of it. To get there, the executive had ignored conventional boundaries, forging and maintaining connections with people in every corner of the organization.

Is social skill considered a key leadership capability in most companies? The answer is yes, especially when compared with the other components of emotional intelligence. People seem to know intuitively that leaders need to manage relationships effectively; no leader is an island. After all, the leader's task is to get work done through other people, and social skill makes that possible. A leader who cannot express her empathy may as well not have it at all. And a leader's motivation will be useless if he cannot communicate his passion to the organization. Social skill allows leaders to put their emotional intelligence to work.

It would be foolish to assert that good-old-fashioned IQ and technical ability are not important ingredients in strong leadership. But the recipe would not be complete without emotional intelligence. It was once thought that the components of emotional intelligence were "nice to have" in business leaders. But now we know that, for the sake of performance, these are ingredients that leaders "need to have."

It is fortunate, then, that emotional intelligence can be learned. The process is not easy. It takes time and, most of all, commitment. But the benefits that come from having a well-developed emotional intelligence, both for the individual and for the organization, make it worth the effort.

Can Emotional Intelligence Be Learned?

FOR AGES, PEOPLE HAVE debated if leaders are born or made. So too goes the debate about emotional intelligence. Are people born with certain levels of empathy, for example, or do they acquire empathy as a result of life's experiences? The answer is both. Scientific inquiry strongly suggests that there is a genetic component to emotional intelligence. Psychological and developmental research indicates that nurture plays a role as well. How much of each perhaps will never be known, but research and practice clearly demonstrate that emotional intelligence can be learned.

One thing is certain: Emotional intelligence increases with age. There is an old-fashioned word for the phenomenon: maturity. Yet even with maturity, some people still need training to enhance their emotional intelligence. Unfortunately, far too many training programs that intend to build leadership skills—including emotional intelligence—are a waste of time and money. The problem is simple: They focus on the wrong part of the brain.

Emotional intelligence is born largely in the neurotransmitters of the brain's limbic system, which governs feelings, impulses, and drives. Research indicates that the limbic system learns best through motivation, extended practice, and feedback. Compare this with the kind of learning that goes on in the neocortex, which governs analytical and technical ability. The neocortex grasps concepts and logic. It is the part of the brain that figures out how to use a computer or make a sales call by reading a book. Not surprisingly—but mistakenly—it is also the part of the brain targeted by most training programs aimed at enhancing emotional intelligence. When such programs take, in effect, a neocortical approach, my research with the Consortium for Research on Emotional Intelligence in Organizations has shown they can even have a *negative* impact on people's job performance.

To enhance emotional intelligence, organizations must refocus their training to include the limbic system. They must help people break old behavioral habits and establish new ones. That not only takes much more time than conventional training programs, it also requires an individualized approach.

Imagine an executive who is thought to be low on empathy by her colleagues. Part of that deficit shows itself as an inability to listen; she interrupts people and doesn't pay close attention to what they're saying. To fix the problem, the executive needs to be motivated to change, and then she needs practice and feedback from others in the company. A colleague or coach could be tapped to let the executive know when she has been observed failing to listen. She would then have to replay the incident and give a better response; that is, demonstrate her ability to absorb what others are saying. And the executive could be directed to observe certain executives who listen well and to mimic their behavior.

With persistence and practice, such a process can lead to lasting results. I know one Wall Street executive who sought to improve his empathy—specifically his ability to read people's reactions and see their perspectives. Before beginning his quest, the executive's subordinates were terrified of working with him. People even went so far as to hide bad news from him. Naturally, he was shocked when finally confronted with these facts. He went home and told his family—but they only confirmed what he had heard at work. When their opinions on any given subject did not mesh with his, they, too, were frightened of him.

Enlisting the help of a coach, the executive went to work to heighten his empathy through practice and feedback. His first step was to take a vacation to a foreign country where he did not speak the language. While there, he monitored his reactions to the unfamiliar and his openness to people who were different from him. When he returned home, humbled by his week abroad, the executive asked his coach to shadow him for parts of the day, several times a week, to critique how he treated people with new or different perspectives. At the same time, he consciously used on-the-job interactions as opportunities to practice "hearing" ideas that differed from his. Finally, the executive had himself videotaped in meetings and asked those who worked for and with him to critique his ability to acknowledge and understand the feelings of others. It took several months, but the executive's emotional intelligence did ultimately rise, and the improvement was reflected in his overall performance on the job.

It's important to emphasize that building one's emotional intelligence cannot—will not—happen without sincere desire and concerted effort. A brief seminar won't help; nor can one buy a how-to manual. It is much harder to learn to empathize—to internalize empathy as a natural response to people—than it is to become adept at regression analysis. But it can be done. "Nothing great was ever achieved without enthusiasm," wrote Ralph Waldo Emerson. If your goal is to become a real leader, these words can serve as a guidepost in your efforts to develop high emotional intelligence.

Originally published in November–December 1998
Reprint R0401H

Narcissistic Leaders

The Incredible Pros,
the Inevitable Cons

MICHAEL MACCOBY

Executive Summary

IN THE WINTER OF 2000, at the height of the dot-com boom, business leaders posed for the covers of *Time*, *BusinessWeek*, and the *Economist* with the aplomb and confidence of rock stars. These were a different breed from their counterparts of just 10 or 20 years before, who shunned the press and whose comments were carefully crafted by corporate PR departments.

Such love of the limelight often stems from what Freud called a narcissistic personality, says psychoanalyst and anthropologist Michael Maccoby in this HBR classic first published in the January–February 2000 issue.

Narcissists are good for companies in extraordinary times, those that need people with the passion and daring to take them in new directions. But narcissists can also lead companies into disaster by refusing to listen to the advice and warnings of their managers. It's not always true, as Andy Grove famously put it, that only the paranoid survive.

Most business advice is focused on the more analytic personality that Freud labeled obsessive. But recommendations about creating teamwork and being more receptive to subordinates will not resonate with narcissists. They didn't get where they are by listening to others, so why should they listen to anyone when they're at the top of their game?

Narcissists who want to overcome the limits of their personalities must work as hard at that as they do at business success. One solution is to find a trusted sidekick, who can point out the operational requirements of the narcissistic leader's often overly grandiose vision and keep him rooted in reality. Another is to take a leap of faith and go into psychoanalysis, which can give these leaders the tools to overcome their sometimes fatal character flaws.

When Michael Maccoby wrote this article, which was first published in early 2000, the business world was still under the spell of the Internet and its revolutionary promise. It was a time, Maccoby wrote, that called for larger-than-life leaders who could see the big picture and paint a compelling portrait of a dramatically different future. And that, he argued, was one reason we saw the emergence of the superstar CEOs—the grandiose, actively self-promoting, and genuinely narcissistic leaders who dominated the covers of business magazines at that time. Skilled orators and creative strategists, narcissists have vision and a great ability to attract and inspire followers.

The times have changed, and we've learned a lot about the dangers of overreliance on big personalities, but that doesn't mean narcissism can't be a useful leadership trait. There's certainly a dark side to narcissism—narcissists, Freud told us, are emotionally isolated and highly distrustful. They're usually poor listeners and lack empathy. Perceived threats can trigger rage. The challenge today— as Maccoby understood it to be four years ago—is to take advantage of their strengths while tempering their weaknesses.

THERE'S SOMETHING NEW and daring about the CEOs who are transforming today's industries. Just compare them with the executives who ran large companies in the 1950s through the 1980s. Those executives shunned the press and had their comments carefully crafted by corporate PR departments. But today's CEOs—superstars such as Bill Gates, Andy Grove, Steve Jobs, Jeff Bezos, and Jack Welch—hire their own publicists, write books, grant spontaneous interviews, and actively promote their personal philosophies. Their faces adorn the covers of magazines like *BusinessWeek, Time,* and the *Economist.* What's more, the world's business personalities are increasingly seen as the makers and shapers of our public and personal agendas. They advise schools on what kids should learn and lawmakers on how to invest the public's money. We look to them for thoughts on everything from the future of e-commerce to hot places to vacation.

There are many reasons today's business leaders have higher profiles than ever before. One is that business plays a much bigger role in our lives than it used to, and its leaders are more often in the limelight. Another is that the business world is experiencing enormous changes that call for visionary and charismatic leadership. But my 25 years of consulting both as a psychoanalyst in private practice and as an adviser to top managers suggest a third reason—namely, a pronounced change in the personality of the strategic leaders at the top. As an anthropologist, I try to understand people in the context in which they operate, and as a psychoanalyst, I tend to see them through a distinctly Freudian lens. Given what I know, I believe that the larger-than-life leaders we are seeing today closely resemble the personality type that Sigmund Freud dubbed narcissistic. "People of this type impress others as being 'personalities,'" he wrote, describing one of the psychological types that clearly fall within the range of normality. "They are especially suited to act as a support for others, to take on the role of leaders, and to give a fresh stimulus to cultural development or damage the established state of affairs."

Throughout history, narcissists have always emerged to inspire people and to shape the future. When military, religious, and political arenas dominated society, it was figures such as Napoléon Bonaparte, Mahatma Gandhi, and Franklin Delano Roosevelt who determined the social agenda. But from time to time, when business became the engine of social change, it, too, generated its share of narcissistic leaders. That was true at the beginning of this century, when men like Andrew Carnegie, John D. Rockefeller, Thomas Edison, and Henry Ford exploited new technologies and restructured American industry. And I think it is true again today.

But Freud recognized that there is a dark side to narcissism. Narcissists, he pointed out, are emotionally isolated and highly distrustful. Perceived threats can trigger rage. Achievements can feed feelings of grandiosity. That's why Freud thought narcissists were the hardest personality types to analyze. Consider how an executive at Oracle describes his narcissistic CEO Larry Ellison: "The difference between God and Larry is that God does not believe he is Larry." That observation is amusing, but it is also troubling. Not surprisingly, most people think of narcissists in a primarily negative way. After all, Freud named the type after the mythical figure Narcissus, who died because of his pathological preoccupation with himself.

Yet narcissism can be extraordinarily useful—even necessary. Freud shifted his views about narcissism over time and recognized that we are all somewhat narcissistic. More recently, psychoanalyst Heinz Kohut built on Freud's theories and developed methods of treating narcissists. Of course, only professional clinicians are trained to tell if narcissism is normal or pathological. In this article, I discuss the differences between productive and unproductive narcissism but do not explore the extreme pathology of borderline conditions and psychosis.

Leaders such as Jack Welch and George Soros are examples of productive narcissists. They are gifted and creative strategists who see the big picture and find meaning in the risky challenge of changing the world and leaving behind a legacy. Indeed, one reason we look to productive narcissists in times of great transition is that they have the audacity to push through the massive transformations that society periodically undertakes. Productive narcissists are not only risk takers willing to get the job done but also charmers who can convert the masses with their rhetoric. The danger is that narcissism can turn unproductive when, lacking self-knowledge and restraining anchors, narcissists become unrealistic dreamers. They nurture grand schemes and harbor the illusion that only circumstances or enemies block their success. This tendency toward grandiosity and distrust is the Achilles' heel of narcissists. Because of it, even brilliant narcissists can come under suspicion for self-involvement, unpredictability, and—in extreme cases—paranoia.

It's easy to see why narcissistic leadership doesn't always mean successful leadership. Consider the case of Volvo's Pehr Gyllenhammar. He had a dream that appealed to a broad international audience—a plan to revolutionize the industrial workplace by replacing the dehumanizing assembly line caricatured in Charlie Chaplin's *Modern Times*. His wildly popular vision called for team-based craftsmanship. Model factories were built and publicized to international acclaim. But his success in pushing through these dramatic changes also sowed the seeds for his downfall. Gyllenhammar started to feel that he could ignore the concerns of his operational managers. He pursued chancy and expensive business deals, which he publicized on television and in the press. On one level, you can ascribe Gyllenhammar's falling out of touch with his workforce simply to faulty strategy. But it is also possible to attribute it to his narcissistic personality. His overestimation of himself led him to believe that others would want him to be the czar of a multinational enterprise. In turn, these fantasies led him to pursue a merger with Renault, which was tremendously unpopular with Swedish employees. Because Gyllenhammar was deaf to complaints about Renault, Swedish managers were forced to take their case public. In the end, shareholders aggressively rejected Gyllenhammar's plan, leaving him with no option but to resign.

Given the large number of narcissists at the helm of corporations today, the challenge facing organizations is to ensure that such leaders do not self-destruct or lead the company to disaster. That can take some doing because it is very hard for narcissists to work through their issues—and virtually impossible for them to do it alone. Narcissists need colleagues and even therapists if they hope to break free from their limitations. But because of their extreme independence and self-protectiveness, it is very difficult to get near them. Kohut maintained that a therapist would have to demonstrate an extraordinarily profound empathic understanding and sympathy for the narcissist's feelings in order to gain his trust. On top of that, narcissists must recognize that they can benefit from such help. For their part, employees must learn how to recognize—and work around—narcissistic bosses. To help them in this endeavor, let's first take a closer look at Freud's theory of personality types.

Three Main Personality Types

While Freud recognized that there are an almost infinite variety of personalities, he identified three main types: erotic, obsessive, and narcissistic. Most of us have elements of all three. We are all, for example, somewhat narcissistic. If that were not so, we would not be able to survive or assert our needs. The point is, one of the dynamic tendencies usually dominates the others, making each of us react differently to success and failure.

Freud's definitions of personality types differed over time. When talking about the erotic personality type, however, Freud generally did not mean a sexual personality but rather one for whom loving and above all being loved is most important. This type of individual is dependent on those people they fear will stop loving them. Many erotics are teachers, nurses, and social workers. At their most productive, they are developers of the young as well as enablers and helpers at work. As managers, they are caring and supportive, but they avoid conflict and make people dependent on them. They are, according to Freud, outer-directed people.

Obsessives, in contrast, are inner-directed. They are self-reliant and conscientious. They create and maintain order and make the most effective operational managers. They look constantly for ways to help people listen better, resolve conflict, and find win-win opportunities. They buy self-improvement books such as Stephen Covey's *The 7 Habits of Highly Effective People*. Obsessives are also ruled by a strict conscience—they like to focus on continuous improvement at work because it fits in with their sense of moral improvement. As entrepreneurs, obsessives start businesses that express their values, but they lack the vision, daring, and charisma it takes to turn a good idea into a great one. The best obsessives set high standards and communicate very effectively. They make sure that instructions are followed and costs are kept within budget. The most productive are great mentors and team players. The unproductive and the uncooperative become narrow experts and rule-bound bureaucrats.

Narcissists, the third type, are independent and not easily impressed. They are innovators, driven in business to gain power and glory. Productive narcissists are experts in their industries, but they go beyond it. They also pose the critical questions. They want to learn everything about everything that affects the company and its products. Unlike erotics, they want to be admired, not loved. And unlike obsessives, they are not troubled by a punishing superego, so they are able to aggressively pursue their goals. Of all the personality types, narcissists run the greatest risk of isolating themselves at the moment of success. And because of their independence and aggressiveness, they are constantly looking out for enemies, sometimes degenerating into paranoia when they are under extreme stress. (For more on personality types, see "Fromm's Fourth Personality Type" at the end of this article.)

Strengths of the Narcissistic Leader

When it comes to leadership, personality type can be instructive. Erotic personalities generally make poor managers—they need too much approval. Obsessives make better leaders—they are your operational managers: critical and cautious. But it is narcissists who come closest to our collective image of great leaders. There are two reasons for this: they have compelling, even gripping, visions for companies, and they have an ability to attract followers.

GREAT VISION

I once asked a group of managers to define a leader. "A person with vision" was a typical response. Productive narcissists understand the vision thing particularly well, because they are by nature people who see the big picture. They are not analyzers who can break up big questions into manageable problems; they aren't number crunchers either (these are usually the obsessives). Nor do they try to extrapolate to understand the future—they attempt to create it. To paraphrase George Bernard Shaw, some people see things, and they say "why?"; narcissists dream things that never were and say, "Why not?"

Consider the difference between Bob Allen, a productive obsessive, and Mike Armstrong, a productive narcissist. In 1997, Allen tried to expand AT&T to reestablish the end-to-end service of the Bell System by reselling local service from the regional Bell operating companies (RBOCs). Although this was a worthwhile endeavor for shareholders and customers, it was hardly earth-shattering. By contrast, through a strategy of combining voice, telecommunications, and Internet access by high-speed broadband telecommunication over cable, Mike Armstrong has "created a new space with his name on it," as one of his colleagues puts it. Armstrong is betting that his costly strategy will beat out the RBOC's less expensive solution of digital sub-scriber lines over copper wire. This example illustrates the different approaches of obsessives and narcissists. The risk Armstrong took is one that few obsessives would feel comfortable taking. His vision is galvanizing AT&T. Who but a narcissistic leader could achieve such a thing? As Napoléon—a classic narcissist—once remarked, "Revolutions are ideal times for soldiers with a lot of wit—and the courage to act."

As in the days of the French Revolution, the world is now changing in astounding ways; narcissists have opportunities they would never have in ordinary times. In short, today's narcissistic leaders have the chance to change the very rules of the game. Consider Robert B. Shapiro, CEO of Monsanto. Shapiro described his vision of genetically modifying crops as "the single most suc-cessful introduction of technology in the history of agri-culture, including the plow" (*New York Times*, August 5, 1999). This is certainly a huge claim—there are still many questions about the safety and public acceptance of genetically engineered fruits and vegetables. But industries like agriculture are desperate for radical change. If Shapiro's gamble is successful, the industry will be transformed in the image of Monsanto. That's why he can get away with painting a picture of Monsanto as a highly profitable "life sciences" company—despite the fact that Monsanto's stock has fallen 12% from 1998 to the end of the third quarter of 1999. (During the same period, the S&P was up 41%.) Unlike Armstrong and Shapiro, it was enough for Bob Allen to win against his competitors in a game measured primarily by the stock market. But narcissistic leaders are after something more. They want—and need—to leave behind a legacy.

SCORES OF FOLLOWERS

Narcissists have vision—but that's not enough. People in mental hospitals also have visions. The simplest definition of a leader is someone whom other people follow. Indeed, narcissists are especially gifted in attracting followers, and more often than not, they do so through language. Narcissists believe that words can move mountains and that inspiring speeches can change people. Narcissistic leaders are often skillful orators, and this is one of the talents that makes them so charismatic. Indeed, anyone who has seen narcissists perform can attest to their personal magnetism and their ability to stir enthusiasm among audiences.

Yet this charismatic gift is more of a two-way affair than most people think. Although it is not always obvious, narcissistic leaders are quite dependent on their followers—they need affirmation, and preferably adulation. Think of Winston Churchill's wartime broadcasts or J.F.K.'s "Ask not what your country can do for you" inaugural address. The adulation that follows from such speeches bolsters the self-confidence and conviction of the speakers. But if no one responds, the narcissist usually becomes insecure, overly shrill, and insistent—just as Ross Perot did.

Even when people respond positively to a narcissist, there are dangers. That's because charisma is a double-edged sword—it fosters both closeness and isolation. As he becomes increasingly self-assured, the narcissist becomes more spontaneous. He feels free of constraints. Ideas flow. He thinks he's invincible. This energy and confidence further inspire his followers. But the very adulation that the narcissist demands can have a corrosive effect. As he expands, he listens even less to words of caution and advice. After all, he has been right before, when others had their doubts. Rather than try to persuade those who disagree with him, he feels justified in ignoring them—creating further isolation. The result is sometimes flagrant risk taking that can lead to catastrophe. In the political realm, there is no clearer example of this than Bill Clinton.

Weaknesses of the Narcissistic Leader

Despite the warm feelings their charisma can evoke, narcissists are typically not comfortable with their own emotions. They listen only for the kind of information they seek. They don't learn easily from others. They don't like to teach but prefer to indoctrinate and make speeches. They dominate meetings with subordinates. The result for the organization is greater internal competitiveness at a time when everyone is already under as much pressure as they can possibly stand. Perhaps the main problem is that the narcissist's faults tend to become even more pronounced as he becomes more successful.

SENSITIVE TO CRITICISM

Because they are extraordinarily sensitive, narcissistic leaders shun emotions as a whole. Indeed, perhaps one of the greatest paradoxes in this age of teamwork and partnering is that the best corporate leader in the contemporary world is the type of person who is emotionally isolated. Narcissistic leaders typically keep others at arm's length. They can put up a wall of defense as thick as the Pentagon. And given their difficulty with knowing or acknowledging their own feelings, they are uncomfortable with other people expressing theirs—especially their negative feelings.

Indeed, even productive narcissists are extremely sensitive to criticism or slights, which feel to them like knives threatening their self-image and their confidence in their visions. Narcissists are almost unimaginably thin-skinned. Like the fairy-tale princess who slept on many mattresses and yet knew she was sleeping on a pea, narcissists—even powerful CEOs—bruise easily. This is one explanation why narcissistic leaders do not want to know what people think of them unless it is causing them a real problem. They cannot tolerate dissent. In fact, they can be extremely abrasive with employees who doubt them or with subordinates who are tough enough to fight back. Steve Jobs, for example, publicly humiliates subordinates. Thus, although narcissistic leaders often say that they want teamwork, what that means in practice is that they want a group of yes-men. As the more independent-minded players leave or are pushed out, succession becomes a particular problem.

POOR LISTENERS

One serious consequence of this oversensitivity to criticism is that narcissistic leaders often do not listen when they feel threatened or attacked. Consider the response of one narcissistic CEO I had worked with for three years who asked me to interview his immediate team and report back to him on what they were thinking. He invited me to his summer home to discuss what I had found. "So what do they think of me?" he asked with seeming nonchalance. "They think you are very creative and courageous," I told him, "but they also feel that you don't listen." "Excuse me, what did you say?" he shot back at once, pretending not to hear. His response was humorous, but it was also tragic.

In a very real way, this CEO could not hear my criticism because it was too painful to tolerate. Some narcissists are so defensive that they go so far as to make a virtue of the fact that they don't listen. As another CEO bluntly put it, "I didn't get here by listening to people!" Indeed, on one occasion when this CEO proposed a daring strategy, none of his subordinates believed it would work. His subsequent success strengthened his conviction that he had nothing to learn about strategy from his lieutenants. But success is no excuse for narcissistic leaders not to listen.

LACK OF EMPATHY

Best-selling business writers today have taken up the slogan of "emotional competencies"—the belief that successful leadership requires a strongly developed sense of empathy. But although they crave empathy from others, productive narcissists are not noted for being particularly empathetic themselves. Indeed, lack of empathy is a characteristic shortcoming of some of the most charismatic and successful narcissists, including Bill Gates and Andy Grove. Of course, leaders do need to communicate persuasively. But a lack of empathy did not prevent some of history's greatest narcissistic leaders from knowing how to communicate—and inspire. Neither Churchill, de Gaulle, Stalin, nor Mao Tse-tung were empathetic. And yet they inspired people because of their passion and their conviction at a time when people longed for certainty.

In fact, in times of radical change, lack of empathy can actually be a strength. A narcissist finds it easier than other personality types to buy and sell companies, to close and move facilities, and to lay off employees— decisions that inevitably make many people angry and sad. But narcissistic leaders typically have few regrets. As one CEO says, "If I listened to my employees' needs and demands, they would eat me alive."

Given this lack of empathy, it's hardly surprising that narcissistic leaders don't score particularly well on evaluations of their interpersonal style. What's more, neither 360-degree evaluations of their management style nor workshops in listening will make them more empathic. Narcissists don't want to change—and as long as they are successful, they don't think they have to. They may see the need for operational managers to get touchy-feely training, but that's not for them.

There is a kind of emotional intelligence associated with narcissists, but it's more street smarts than empathy. Narcissistic leaders are acutely aware of whether or not people are with them wholeheartedly. They know whom they can use. They can be brutally exploitative. That's why, even though narcissists undoubtedly have "star quality," they are often unlikable. They easily stir up people against them, and it is only in tumultuous times, when their gifts are desperately needed, that people are willing to tolerate narcissists as leaders.

DISTASTE FOR MENTORING

Lack of empathy and extreme independence make it difficult for narcissists to mentor and be mentored. Generally speaking, narcissistic leaders set very little store by mentoring. They seldom mentor others, and when they do they typically want their protégés to be pale reflections of themselves. Even those narcissists like Jack Welch who are held up as strong mentors are usually more interested in instructing than in coaching.

Narcissists certainly don't credit mentoring or educational programs for their own development as leaders. A few narcissistic leaders such as Bill Gates may find a friend or consultant—for instance, Warren Buffett, a superproductive obsessive—whom they can trust to be their guide and confidant. But most narcissists prefer "mentors" they can control. A 32-year-old marketing vice president, a narcissist with CEO potential, told me that she had rejected her boss as a mentor. As she put it, "First of all, I want to keep the relationship at a distance. I don't want to be influenced by emotions. Second, there are things I don't want him to know. I'd rather hire an outside consultant to be my coach." Although narcissistic leaders appear to be at ease with others, they find intimacy—which is a prerequisite for mentoring—to be difficult. Younger narcissists will establish peer relations with authority rather than seek a parentlike mentoring relationship. They want results and are willing to take chances arguing with authority.

AN INTENSE DESIRE TO COMPETE

Narcissistic leaders are relentless and ruthless in their pursuit of victory. Games are not games but tests of their survival skills. Of course, all successful managers want to win, but narcissists are not restrained by conscience. Organizations led by narcissists are generally characterized by intense internal competition. Their passion to win is marked by both the promise of glory and the primitive danger of extinction. It is a potent brew that energizes companies, creating a sense of urgency, but it can also be dangerous. These leaders see everything as a threat. As Andy Grove puts it, brilliantly articulating the narcissist's fear, distrust, and aggression, "Only the paranoid survive." The concern, of course, is that the narcissist finds enemies that aren't there—even among his colleagues. (See "The Rise and Fall of a Narcissist" at the end of this article for a true story of failure.)

Avoiding the Traps

There is very little business literature that tells narcissistic leaders how to avoid the pitfalls. There are two reasons for this. First, relatively few narcissistic leaders are interested in looking inward. And second, psychoanalysts don't usually get close enough to them, especially in the workplace, to write about them. (The noted psychoanalyst Harry Levinson is an exception.) As a result, advice on leadership focuses on obsessives, which explains why so much of it is about creating teamwork and being more receptive to subordinates. But as we've already seen, this literature is of little interest to narcissists, nor is it likely to help subordinates understand their narcissistic leaders. The absence of managerial literature on narcissistic leaders doesn't mean that it is impossible to devise strategies for dealing with narcissism. In the course of a long career counseling CEOs, I have identified three basic ways in which productive narcissists can avoid the traps of their own personality.

FIND A TRUSTED SIDEKICK

Many narcissists can develop a close relationship with one person, a sidekick who acts as an anchor, keeping the narcissistic partner grounded. However, given that narcissistic leaders trust only their own insights and view of reality, the sidekick has to understand the narcissistic leader and what he is trying to achieve. The narcissist must feel that this person, or in some cases persons, is practically an extension of himself. The sidekick must also be sensitive enough to manage the relationship. Don Quixote is a classic example of a narcissist who was out of touch with reality but who was constantly saved from disaster by his squire Sancho Panza. Not surprisingly, many narcissistic leaders rely heavily on their spouses, the people they are closest to. But dependence on spouses can be risky, because they may further isolate the narcissistic leader from his company by supporting his grandiosity and feeding his paranoia. I once knew a CEO in this kind of relationship with his spouse. He took to accusing loyal subordinates of plotting against him just because they ventured a few criticisms of his ideas.

It is much better for a narcissistic leader to choose a colleague as his sidekick. Good sidekicks are able to point out the operational requirements of the narcissistic leader's vision and keep him rooted in reality. The best sidekicks are usually productive obsessives. Gyllenhammar, for instance, was most effective at Volvo when he had an obsessive COO, Håkan Frisinger, to focus on improving quality and cost, as well as an obsessive HR director, Berth Jönsson, to implement his vision. Similarly, Bill Gates can think about the future from the stratosphere because Steve Ballmer, a tough obsessive president, keeps the show on the road. At Oracle, CEO Larry Ellison can afford to miss key meetings and spend time on his boat contemplating a future without PCs because he has a productive obsessive COO in Ray Lane to run the company for him. But the job of sidekick entails more than just executing the leader's ideas. The sidekick also has to get his leader to accept new ideas. To do this, he must be able to show the leader how the new ideas fit with his views and serve his interests. (For more on dealing with narcissistic bosses, see "Working for a Narcissist" at the end of this article.)

INDOCTRINATE THE ORGANIZATION

The narcissistic CEO wants all his subordinates to think the way he does about the business. Productive narcissists—people who often have a dash of the obsessive personality—are good at converting people to their point of view. One of the most successful at this is GE's Jack Welch. Welch uses toughness to build a corporate culture and to implement a daring business strategy, including the buying and selling of scores of companies. Unlike other narcissistic leaders such as Gates, Grove, and Ellison, who have transformed industries with new products, Welch was able to transform his industry by focusing on execution and pushing companies to the limits of quality and efficiency, bumping up revenues and wringing out costs. In order to do so, Welch hammers out a huge corporate culture in his own image—a culture that provides impressive rewards for senior managers and shareholders.

Welch's approach to culture building is widely misunderstood. Many observers, notably Noel Tichy in *The Leadership Engine*, argue that Welch forms his company's leadership culture through teaching. But Welch's "teaching" involves a personal ideology that he indoctrinates into GE managers through speeches, memos, and confrontations. Rather than create a dialogue, Welch makes pronouncements (either be the number one or two company in your market or get out), and he institutes programs (such as Six Sigma quality) that become the GE party line. Welch's strategy has been extremely effective. GE managers must either internalize his vision, or they must leave. Clearly, this is incentive learning with a vengeance. I would even go so far as to call Welch's teaching brainwashing. But Welch does have the rare insight and know-how to achieve what all narcissistic business leaders are trying to do—namely, get the organization to identify with them, to think the way they do, and to become the living embodiment of their companies.

GET INTO ANALYSIS

Narcissists are often more interested in controlling others than in knowing and disciplining themselves. That's why, with very few exceptions, even productive narcissists do not want to explore their personalities with the help of insight therapies such as psychoanalysis. Yet since Heinz Kohut, there has been a radical shift in psychoanalytic thinking about what can be done to help narcissists work through their rage, alienation, and grandiosity. Indeed, if they can be persuaded to undergo therapy, narcissistic leaders can use tools such as psychoanalysis to overcome vital character flaws.

Consider the case of one exceptional narcissistic CEO who asked me to help him understand why he so often lost his temper with subordinates. He lived far from my home city, and so the therapy was sporadic and very unorthodox. Yet he kept a journal of his dreams, which we interpreted together either by phone or when we met. Our analysis uncovered painful feelings of being unappreciated that went back to his inability to impress a cold father. He came to realize that he demanded an unreasonable amount of praise and that when he felt unappreciated by his subordinates, he became furious. Once he understood that, he was able to recognize his narcissism and even laugh about it. In the middle of our work, he even announced to his top team that I was psychoanalyzing him and asked them what they thought of that. After a pregnant pause, one executive vice president piped up, "Whatever you're doing, you should keep doing it, because you don't get so angry anymore." Instead of being trapped by narcissistic rage, this CEO was learning how to express his concerns constructively.

Leaders who can work on themselves in that way tend to be the most productive narcissists. In addition to being self-reflective, they are also likely to be open, likable, and good-humored. Productive narcissists have perspective; they are able to detach themselves and laugh at their irrational needs. Although serious about achieving their goals, they are also playful. As leaders, they are aware of being performers. A sense of humor helps them maintain enough perspective and humility to keep on learning.

The Best and Worst of Times

As I have pointed out, narcissists thrive in chaotic times. In more tranquil times and places, however, even the most brilliant narcissist will seem out of place. In his short story *The Curfew Tolls*, Stephen Vincent Benét speculates on what would have happened to Napoléon if he had been born some 30 years earlier. Retired in pre-revolutionary France, Napoléon is depicted as a lonely artillery major boasting to a vacationing British general about how he could have beaten the English in India. The point, of course, is that a visionary born in the wrong time can seem like a pompous buffoon.

Historically, narcissists in large corporations have been confined to sales positions, where they use their persuasiveness and imagination to best effect. In settled times, the problematic side of the narcissistic personality usually conspires to keep narcissists in their place, and they can typically rise to top management positions only by starting their own companies or by leaving to lead upstarts. Consider Joe Nacchio, formerly in charge of both the business and consumer divisions of AT&T. Nacchio was a supersalesman and a popular leader in the mid-1990s. But his desire to create a new network for business customers was thwarted by colleagues who found him abrasive, self-promoting, and ruthlessly ambitious.

Two years ago, Nacchio left AT&T to become CEO of Qwest, a company that is creating a long-distance fiber-optic cable network. Nacchio had the credibility—and charisma—to sell Qwest's initial public offering to financial markets and gain a high valuation. Within a short space of time, he turned Qwest into an attractive target for the RBOCs, which were looking to move into long-distance telephony and Internet services. Such a sale would have given Qwest's owners a handsome profit on their investment. But Nacchio wanted more. He wanted to expand—to compete with AT&T—and for that he needed local service. Rather than sell Qwest, he chose to make a bid himself for local telephone operator U.S. West, using Qwest's highly valued stock to finance the deal. The market voted on this display of expansiveness with its feet—Qwest's stock price fell 40% between last June, when he made the deal, and the end of the third quarter of 1999. (The S&P index dropped 5.7% during the same period.)

Like other narcissists, Nacchio likes risk—and sometimes ignores the costs. But with the dramatic discontinuities going on in the world today, more and more large corporations are getting into bed with narcissists. They are finding that there is no substitute for narcissistic leaders in an age of innovation. Companies need leaders who do not try to anticipate the future so much as create it. But narcissistic leaders—even the most productive of them—can self-destruct and lead their organizations terribly astray. For companies whose narcissistic leaders recognize their limitations, these will be the best of times. For other companies, these could turn out to be the worst.

Fromm's Fourth Personality Type

NOT LONG AFTER FREUD described his three personality types in 1931, psychoanalyst Erich Fromm proposed a fourth personality type, which has become particularly prevalent in today's service economy. Fromm called this type the "marketing personality," and it is exemplified by the lead character in Woody Allen's movie *Zelig*, a man so governed by his need to be valued that he becomes exactly like the people he happens to be around.

Marketing personalities are more detached than erotics and so are less likely to cement close ties. They are also less driven by conscience than obsessives. Instead, they are motivated by a radarlike anxiety that permeates everything they do. Because they are so eager to please and to alleviate this anxiety, marketing personalities excel at selling themselves to others.

Unproductive marketing types lack direction and the ability to commit themselves to people or projects. But when productive, marketing types are good at facilitating teams and keeping the focus on adding value as defined by customers and colleagues. Like obsessives, marketing personalities are avid consumers of self-help books. Like narcissists, they are not wedded to the past. But marketing types generally make poor leaders in times of crisis. They lack the daring needed to innovate and are too responsive to current, rather than future, customer demands.

The Rise and Fall of a Narcissist

THE STORY OF JAN CARLZON, the former CEO of the Scandinavian airline SAS, is an almost textbook example of how a narcissist's weaknesses can cut short a brilliant career. In the 1980s, Carlzon's vision of SAS as the businessperson's airline was widely acclaimed in the business press; management guru Tom Peters described him as a model leader. In 1989, when I first met Carlzon and his management team, he compared the ideal organization to the Brazilian soccer team—in principle, there would be no fixed roles, only innovative plays. I asked the members of the management team if they agreed with this vision of an empowered front line. One vice president, a former pilot, answered no. "I still believe that the best organization is the military," he said. I then asked Carlzon for his reaction to that remark. "Well," he replied, "that may be true, if your goal is to shoot your customers."

That rejoinder was both witty and dismissive; clearly, Carlzon was not engaging in a serious dialogue with his subordinates. Nor was he listening to other advisers. Carlzon ignored the issue of high costs, even when many observers pointed out that SAS could not compete without improving productivity. He threw money at expensive acquisitions of hotels and made an unnecessary investment in Continental Airlines just months before it declared bankruptcy.

Carlzon's story perfectly corroborates the often-recorded tendency of narcissists to become overly expansive—and hence isolated—at the very pinnacle of their success. Seduced by the flattery he received in the international press, Carlzon's self-image became so enormously inflated that his feet left the ground. And given his vulnerability to grandiosity, he was propelled by a need to expand his organization rather than develop it. In due course, as Carlzon led the company deeper and deeper into losses, he was fired. Now he is a venture capitalist helping budding companies. And SAS has lost its glitter.

Working for a Narcissist

DEALING WITH A NARCISSISTIC BOSS isn't easy. You have to be prepared to look for another job if your boss becomes too narcissistic to let you disagree with him. But remember that the company is typically betting on *his* vision of the future—not yours. Here are a few tips on how to survive in the short term:

Always empathize with your boss's feelings, but don't expect any empathy back

Look elsewhere for your own self-esteem. Understand that behind his display of infallibility, there hides a deep vulnerability. Praise his achievements and reinforce his best impulses, but don't be shamelessly sycophantic. An intelligent narcissist can see through flatterers and prefers independent people who truly appreciate him. Show that you will protect his image, inside and outside the company. But be careful if he asks for an honest evaluation. What he wants is information that will help him solve a problem about his image. He will resent any honesty that threatens his inflated self-image and will likely retaliate.

Give your boss ideas, but always let him take the credit for them

Find out what he thinks before presenting your views. If you believe he is wrong, show how a different approach would be in his best interest. Take his paranoid views seriously, don't brush them aside—they often reveal sharp intuitions. Disagree only when you can demonstrate how he will benefit from a different point of view.

Hone your time-management skills

Narcissistic leaders often give subordinates many more orders than they can possibly execute. Ignore the requests he makes that don't make sense. Forget about them. He will. But be careful: carve out free time for yourself only when you know there's a lull in the boss's schedule. Narcissistic leaders feel free to call you at any hour of the day or night. Make yourself available, or be prepared to get out.

Originally published in January–February 2000
Reprint R0401J

Understanding Leadership

W.C.H. PRENTICE

Executive Summary

THE WOULD-BE ANALYST of leadership usually studies popularity, power, showmanship, or wisdom in long-range planning. But none of these qualities is the essence of leadership. Leadership is the accomplishment of a goal through the direction of human assistants—a human and social achievement that stems from the leader's understanding of his or her fellow workers and the relationship of their individual goals to the group's aim.

To be successful, leaders must learn two basic lessons: People are complex, and people are different. Human beings respond not only to the traditional carrot and stick but also to ambition, patriotism, love of the good and the beautiful, boredom, self-doubt, and many other desires and emotions. One person may find satisfaction in solving intellectual problems but may never be given the opportunity to explore how that satisfaction can be applied to business. Another may need a friendly, admiring relationship and may be constantly frustrated by the failure of his superior to recognize and take advantage of that need.

In this article, first published in HBR's September–October 1961 issue, W.C.H. Prentice argues that by responding to such individual patterns, the leader will be able to create genuinely intrinsic interest in the work. Ideally, Prentice says, managerial dominions should be small enough that every supervisor can know those who report to him or her as human beings.

Prentice calls for democratic leadership that, without creating anarchy, gives employees opportunities to learn and grow. This concept, along with his rejection of the notion that leadership is the exercise of power or the possession of extraordinary analytical skill, foreshadows the work of more recent authors such as Abraham Zaleznik and Daniel Goleman, who have fundamentally changed the way we look at leadership.

Although the more recent work of authors such as Abraham Zaleznik and Daniel Goleman has fundamentally changed the way we look at leadership, many of their themes were foreshadowed in W.C.H. Prentice's 1961 article rejecting the notion of leadership as the exercise of power and force or the possession of extraordinary analytical skill. Prentice defined leadership as "the accomplishment of a goal through the direction of human assistants" and a successful leader as one who can understand people's motivations and enlist employee participation in a way that marries individual needs and interests to the group's purpose. He called for democratic leadership that gives employees opportunities to learn and grow—without creating anarchy. While his language in some passages is dated, Prentice's observations on how leaders can motivate employees to support the organization's goals are timeless, and they were remarkably prescient.

A̲TTEMPTS TO ANALYZE leadership tend to fail because the would-be analyst misconceives his task. He usually does not study leadership at all. Instead he studies popularity, power, showmanship, or wisdom in long-range planning. Some leaders have these things, but they are not of the essence of leadership.

Leadership is the accomplishment of a goal through the direction of human assistants. The man who successfully marshals his human collaborators to achieve particular ends is a leader. A great leader is one who can do so day after day, and year after year, in a wide variety of circumstances.

He may not possess or display power; force or the threat of harm may never enter into his dealings. He may not be popular; his followers may never do what he wishes out of love or admiration for him. He may not ever be a colorful person; he may never use memorable devices to dramatize the purposes of his group or to focus attention on his leadership. As for the important matter of setting goals, he may actually be a man of little influence, or even of little skill; as a leader he may merely carry out the plans of others.

His *unique* achievement is a human and social one which stems from his understanding of his fellow workers and the relationship of their individual goals to the group goal that he must carry out.

Problems and Illusions

It is not hard to state in a few words what successful leaders do that makes them effective. But it is much harder to tease out the components that determine their success. The usual method is to provide adequate recognition of each worker's function so that he can foresee the satisfaction of some major interest or motive of his in the carrying out of the group enterprise. Crude forms of leadership rely solely on single sources of satisfaction such as monetary rewards or the alleviation of fears about various kinds of insecurity. The task is adhered to because following orders will lead to a paycheck, and deviation will lead to unemployment.

No one can doubt that such forms of motivation are effective within limits. In a mechanical way they do attach the worker's self-interest to the interest of the employer or the group. But no one can doubt the weaknesses of such simple techniques. Human beings are not machines with a single set of push buttons. When their complex responses to love, prestige, independence, achievement, and group membership are unrecognized on the job, they perform at best as automata who bring far less than their maximum efficiency to the task, and at worst as rebellious slaves who consciously or unconsciously sabotage the activities they are supposed to be furthering.

It is ironic that our basic image of "the leader" is so often that of a military commander, because—most of the time, at least—military organizations are the purest example of an unimaginative application of simple reward and punishment as motivating devices. The invention in World War II of the term "snafu" (situation normal, all fouled up) merely epitomizes what literature about military life from Greece and Rome to the present day has amply recorded; namely, that in no other human endeavor is morale typically so poor or goldbricking and waste so much in evidence.

In defense of the military, two observations are relevant:

1. The military undeniably has special problems. Because men get killed and have to be replaced, there are important reasons for treating them uniformly and mechanically.

2. Clarity about duties and responsibilities, as maximized by the autocratic chain of command, is not only essential to warfare but has undoubted importance for most group enterprises. In fact, any departure from an essentially military type of leadership is still considered in some circles a form of anarchy.

We have all heard the cry, "somebody's got to be the boss," and I suppose no one would seriously disagree. But it is dangerous to confuse the chain of command or table of organization with a method of getting things done. It is instead comparable to the diagram of a football play which shows a general plan and how each individual contributes to it.

The diagram is not leadership. By itself it has no bearing one way or another on how well executed the play will be. Yet that very question of effective execution is the problem of leadership. Rewards and threats may help each player to carry out his assignment, but in the long run if success is to be continuing and if morale is to survive, each player must not only fully understand his part and its relation to the group effort; he must also *want* to carry it out. The problem of every leader is to create these wants and to find ways to channel existing wants into effective cooperation.

Relations with People

When the leader succeeds, it will be because he has learned two basic lessons: Men are complex, and men are different. Human beings respond not only to the traditional carrot and stick used by the driver of a donkey but also to ambition, patriotism, love of the good and the beautiful, boredom, self-doubt, and many more dimensions and patterns of thought and feeling that make them men. But the strength and importance of these interests are not the same for every worker, nor is the degree to which they can be satisfied in his job. For example:

- One man may be characterized primarily by a deep religious need but find that fact quite irrelevant to his daily work.

- Another may find his main satisfactions in solving intellectual problems and never be led to discover how his love for chess problems and mathematical puzzles can be applied to his business.

- Or still another may need a friendly, admiring relationship that he lacks at home and be constantly frustrated by the failure of his superior to recognize and take advantage of that need.

To the extent that the leader's circumstances and skill permit him to respond to such individual patterns, he will be better able to create genuinely intrinsic interest in the work that he is charged with getting done. And in the last analysis an ideal organization should have workers at every level reporting to someone whose dominion is small enough to enable him to know as human beings those who report to him.

Limits of the Golden Rule

Fortunately, the prime motives of people who live in the same culture are often very much alike, and there are some general motivational rules that work very well indeed. The effectiveness of Dale Carnegie's famous prescriptions in his *How to Win Friends and Influence People* is a good example. Its major principle is a variation of the Golden Rule: "treat others as you would like to be treated." While limited and oversimplified, such a rule is a great improvement over the primitive coercive approaches or the straight reward-for-desired-behavior approach.

But it would be a great mistake not to recognize that some of the world's most ineffective leadership comes from the "treat others as you would be treated" school. All of us have known unselfish people who earnestly wished to satisfy the needs of their fellows but who were nevertheless completely inept as executives (or perhaps even as friends or as husbands), because it never occurred to them that others had tastes or emotional requirements different from their own. We all know the tireless worker who recognizes no one else's fatigue or boredom, the barroom-story addict who thinks it jolly to regale even the ladies with his favorite anecdotes, the devotee of public service who tries to win friends and influence people by offering them tickets to lectures on missionary work in Africa, the miserly man who thinks everyone is after money, and so on.

Leadership really does require more subtlety and per-ceptiveness than is implied in the saying, "Do as you would be done by."

The one who leads us effectively must seem to under-stand our goals and purposes. He must seem to be in a position to satisfy them; he must seem to understand the implications of his own actions; he must seem to be con-sistent and clear in his decisions. The word "seem" is important here. If we do not apprehend the would-be leader as one who has these traits, it will make no differ-ence how able he may really be. We will still not follow his lead. If, on the other hand, we have been fooled and he merely seems to have these qualities, we will still fol-low him until we discover our error. In other words, it is the impression he makes at any one time that will deter-mine the influence he has on his followers.

Pitfalls of Perception

For followers to recognize their leader as he really is may be as difficult as it is for him to understand them com-pletely. Some of the worst difficulties in relationships between superiors and subordinates come from misper-ceiving reality. So much of what we understand in the world around us is colored by the conceptions and preju-dices we start with. My view of my employer or superior may be so colored by expectations based on the behavior of other bosses that facts may not appear in the same way to him and to me. Many failures of leadership can be traced to oversimplified misperceptions on the part of the worker or to failures of the superior to recognize the context or frame of reference within which his actions will be understood by the subordinate.

A couple of examples of psychological demonstra-tions from the work of S.E. Asch[1] will illustrate this point:

- If I describe a man as warm, intelligent, ambitious, and thoughtful, you get one kind of picture of him. But if I describe another person as cold, ambitious, thoughtful, and intelligent, you probably get a picture of a very different sort of man. Yet I have merely changed one word and the order of a couple of others. The kind of preparation that one adjective gives for those that follow is tremendously effective in determining what meaning will be given to them. The term "thoughtful" may mean thoughtful of others or perhaps rational when it is applied to a warm person toward whom we have already accepted a positive orientation. But as applied to a cold man the same term may mean brooding, calculating, plotting. We must learn to be aware of the degree to which one set of observations about a man may lead us to erroneous conclusions about his other behavior.

- Suppose that I show two groups of observers a film of an exchange of views between an employer and his subordinate. The scene portrays disagreement followed by anger and dismissal. The blame for the difficulty will be assigned very differently by the two groups if I have shown one a scene of the worker earlier in a happy, loving family breakfast setting, while the other group has seen instead a breakfast-table scene where the worker snarls at his family and storms out of the house. The altercation will be understood altogether differently by people who have had favorable or unfavorable glimpses of the character in question.

In business, a worker may perceive an offer of increased authority as a dangerous removal from the safety of assured, though gradual, promotion. A change in channels of authority or reporting, no matter how valuable in increasing efficiency, may be thought of as a personal challenge or affront. The introduction of a labor-saving process may be perceived as a threat to one's job. An invitation to discuss company policy may be perceived as an elaborate trap to entice one into admitting heretical or disloyal views. A new fringe benefit may be regarded as an excuse not to pay higher salaries. And so on.

Too often, the superior is entirely unprepared for these interpretations, and they seem to him stupid, dishonest, or perverse—or all three. But the successful leader will have been prepared for such responses. He will have known that many of his workers have been brought up to consider their employers as their natural enemies, and that habit has made it second nature for them to "act like an employee" in this respect and always to be suspicious of otherwise friendly overtures from above.

The other side of the same situation is as bad. The habit of acting like a boss can be destructive, too. For instance, much resistance to modern concepts of industrial relations comes from employers who think such ideas pose too great a threat to the long-established picture of themselves as business autocrats. Their image makes progress in labor relations difficult.

Troubles of a Subordinate

But another and still more subtle factor may intervene between employer and employee—a factor that will be recognized and dealt with by successful industrial leaders. That factor is the psychological difficulty of being a subordinate. It is not easy to be a subordinate. If I take orders from another, it limits the scope of my independent decision and judgment; certain areas are established within which I do what he wishes instead of what I wish. To accept such a role without friction or rebellion, I must find in it a reflection of some form of order that goes beyond my own personal situation (i.e., my age, class, rank, and so forth), or perhaps find that the balance of dependence and independence actually suits my needs. These two possibilities lead to different practical consequences.

For one thing, it is harder to take orders from one whom I do not consider in some sense superior. It is true that one of the saddest failures in practical leadership may be the executive who tries so hard to be one of the boys that he destroys any vestige of awe that his workers might have had for him, with the consequence that they begin to see him as a man like themselves and to wonder why they should take orders from him. An understanding leader will not let his workers think that he considers them inferiors, but he may be wise to maintain a kind of psychological distance that permits them to accept his authority without resentment.

When one of two people is in a superior position and must make final decisions, he can hardly avoid frustrating the aims of the subordinate, at least on occasion. And frustration seems to lead to aggression. That is, thwarting brings out a natural tendency to fight back. It does not take much thwarting to build up a habit of being ready to attack or defend oneself when dealing with the boss.

The situation is made worse if the organization is such that open anger toward the boss is unthinkable, for then the response to frustration is itself frustrated, and a vicious cycle is started. Suggestion boxes, grievance committees, departmental rivalries, and other such devices may serve as lightning rods for the day-to-day hostility engendered by the frustrations inherent in being a subordinate. But in the long run an effective leader will be aware of the need to balance dependence with independence, constraint with autonomy, so that the inevitable psychological consequences of taking orders do not loom too large.

Better yet, he will recognize that many people are frightened by complete independence and need to feel the security of a system that prescribes limits to their freedom. He will try to adjust the amounts and kinds of freedom to fit the psychological needs of his subordinates. Generally this means providing a developmental program in which the employee can be given some sense of where he is going within the company, and the effective leader will make sure that the view is a realistic one. Here an analogy may be helpful:

Nothing is more destructive of morale in any group situation than a phony democracy of the kind one finds in some families. Parents who announce that the children are going to participate share-and-share-alike in all decisions soon find that they cannot, in fact, let them, and when the program fails, the children are especially thwarted. They come to perceive each of the necessarily frequent decisions that are not made by vote or consultation as arbitrary. They develop a strong sense of injustice and rebellion.

In industry the same conditions hold. It is no good to pretend that certain decisions can be made by subordinates if in fact they cannot. To make dependency tolerable, the lines must be clearly drawn between those decisions that are the prerogative of the superior and those that can be made by or in consultation with the subordinate. Once those lines have been drawn, it is essential not to transgress them any more often than is absolutely necessary.

Ideally, the subordinate should have an area within which he is free to operate without anyone looking over his shoulder. The superior should clarify the goals and perhaps suggest alternative ways of achieving them, but the subordinate should feel free to make the necessary choices. That ideal may sound artificial to autocrats of "the old school," and, if it does, it will mean nothing even if they give lip service to it. If the worker knows that the boss likes plan A, he is not going to try plan B and risk his job if it fails. If he knows that his job rides on every major decision, he can only play safe by identifying himself in every case with his superior's views. But that makes him an automaton who can bring no additional intelligence to the organization nor free his superiors from any decisions. He earns the respect of no one—not even the boss who helped make him that way.

Goals in Development

No decision is worth the name unless it involves the balancing of risks and returns. If it were a sure thing, we would not need a man to use his judgment about it. Mistakes are inevitable. What we must expect of employees is that they learn from their mistakes, not that they never make them. It should be the executive's concern to watch the long-term growth of his men to see that, as they learn, their successes increasingly outweigh their failures.

This concept of long-run growth is a vital part of continuing leadership. Each man must be permitted to know that his role in the group is subject to development and that its development is limited only by his contributions. Especially, he must see the leader as the man most interested in and helpful toward his growth. It is not enough to have interested personnel officers or other staff people who play no role in policy making. Despite all the assistance they can render in technical ways, they can never take the place of an interest on the part of the responsible executive.

Dealing with Tact

At just this point, one often finds misconceptions. No sensible person wishes to make of the executive a substitute for father or psychiatrist or even director of personnel. His interest can and should be entirely impersonal and unsentimental. He might put it to the employee somewhat as follows:

> *There is nothing personal about this. Anyone in your post would get the same treatment. But as long as you work for me, I am going to see that you get every opportunity to use your last ounce of potential. Your growth and satisfaction are a part of my job. The faster you develop into a top contributor to this company, the better I will like it. If you see a better way to do your job, do it that way; if something is holding you back, come and see me about it. If you are right, you will get all the help I can give you plus the recognition you deserve.*

To genuine growth of an employee will occur without some teaching. The superior must from time to time take cognizance of the successes and failures and make sure that the subordinate sees them and their consequences as he does. And at this point of assessment a gravely difficult aspect of leadership arises. How can criticism be impersonal and still effective? How can a decision or a method be criticized without the worker feeling that he is personally being demeaned?

The importance of adequate communication at this point is twofold. Not only may long-range damage be done to employee morale, but a quite specific short-range effect is often the employee's failure to do what he should toward carrying out the boss's alternative plan, since its failure might prove that he had been right in the first place. It is all too easy for a leader to produce antagonism and defensiveness by dealing impersonally with a problem and forgetting the human emotions and motives that are involved in it.

Interestingly enough, such failures seem to happen more often in office situations than anywhere else, and we might well wonder if we have not tended to insulate behavior in management from behavior outside—in the home, for instance. We do not assume that an order or a memorandum is the best way of making our wishes acceptable at home. Most reasonably bright people learn early in life how to get others to cooperate. It is second nature to create a personal and emotional setting that is right for the particular person (e.g., wife, adult son, teenage daughter, or child) and for the particular request that is to be made.

More than that, we are likely to know which aspects of, say, a vacation plan to stress to make it seem attractive to the wife who wants to be waited on, the son who wants to fish, or the daughter who wants adolescent companions. We are likely to learn, too, that one of these may be more readily persuaded if she has a hand in the decision-making process, while another wishes only to have a ready-made plan submitted for his approval or disdain. Indeed, we probably respond to such differences at home with very little thought.

But in the office we lay aside our everyday intuitive skills in human relations and put on the mask of an employer or an executive. We try to handle our tasks with orders or directives impersonally aimed at whoever happens to be responsible for their execution, forgetting that effective mobilization of human resources always requires the voluntary participation of all. Leadership is an interaction among people. It requires followers with particular traits and particular skills and a leader who knows how to use them.

Secrets of a Symphony Orchestra Conductor

The director of an orchestra may perhaps serve as a useful model for some of the important relationships which run through all leadership situations:

1. Obvious enough in this context, but not always remembered, is the fact that the men must have the requisite skills and training for their roles. Not all group failures are the boss's fault. Toscanini could not get great music from a high-school band.

2. A psychological setting must be established for the common task. A conductor must set up his ground rules, his signals, and his tastes in such a way that the mechanics of getting a rehearsal started do not interfere with the musical purpose. Just as the conductor must establish agreement about promptness at rehearsals, talking or smoking between numbers, new versus old music, and a dozen other things that might otherwise come between him and his col-

leagues in their common aim, so every office or factory must have rules or customs which are clearly understood and easily followed.

3. Most important of all, the musicians must share satisfaction with their leader in the production of music or of music of a certain quality. Unless they individually achieve a sense of accomplishment or even fulfillment, his leadership has failed and he will not make great music. Some distinguished conductors have been petty tyrants; others play poker with their musicians and become godfathers to their babies. These matters are essentially irrelevant. What the great conductor achieves is each instrumentalist's conviction that he is taking part in the making of a kind of music that could only be made under such a leader. Personal qualities and mannerisms may have a secondary importance; they may serve as reminders, reinstating and reinforcing the vital image of a man with the highest musical standards. But no one can become a Toscanini by imitating his mannerisms.

"Low-Pressure" Leadership

These simple facts are often overlooked. In industry we can find endless numbers of executives who merely mimic the surface characteristics of some successful colleague or superior without ever trying to find ways to enlist the active participation of their own staffs by showing them ways to personal fulfillment in the common task.

These executives take the approach that a certain type of salesman takes; and it is significant, I think, that the financial, manufacturing, and research staffs of many companies look on salesmen as a necessary evil, and would be horrified at the thought of bringing what they consider a "sales approach" into management. Their reason may never be clearly formulated, but it surely has something to do with an air of trickery and manipulation that surrounds some advertising, marketing, and selling. The salesmen and advertisers I refer to are often willing to seek and exploit a weak point in their customer's defenses and make a sale even when they suspect or perhaps know that the customer will live to regret the purchase.

Slick uses of social and psychological tricks can indeed result in persuading another to do your bidding, but they are unfit for a continuing human relationship. As every truly constructive salesman knows, a business transaction should benefit both buyer and seller. And that means finding out the needs of the customer, making sure that he understands them himself, and providing him with a product that will satisfy that need. Trained in such an approach, the salesman should be the executive par excellence, carrying over into administrative dealings with people what he has been using in sales.

By contrast, the tricky, fast-talking manipulator who prides himself on outwitting his customers, who counts on selling a man cigarettes by playing on his vanity or selling a woman cosmetics by playing on her ambition, might turn into an executive with the same contempt for his workers that he had previously for his customers. If he enjoys hoodwinking his workers by playing on their motives and their interests, they will soon discover that they are being toyed with, and the loyalty and confidence that are an essential ingredient of effective leadership will be corroded away.

Conclusion

In the last resort, an executive must use his skills and his human insight as does an orchestra leader—to capture individual satisfactions in the common enterprise and to create fulfillment that holds the subordinate to his part. No collection of cute tricks of enticement or showmanship can do that for him.

Leadership, despite what we sometimes think, consists of a lot more than just "understanding people," "being nice to people," or not "pushing other people around." Democracy is sometimes thought to imply no division of authority, or to imply that everyone can be his own boss. Of course, that is nonsense, especially in business. But business leadership can be democratic in the sense of providing the maximum opportunity for growth to each worker without creating anarchy.

In fact, the orderly arrangement of functions and the accurate perception of a leader's role in that arrangement must always precede the development of his abilities to the maximum. A leader's job is to provide that recognition of roles and functions within the group that will permit each member to satisfy and fulfill some major motive or interest.

Notes

1. "Forming Impressions of Personality," *The Journal of Abnormal and Social Psychology*, 1946.

Originally published in September–October 1961
Reprint R0401K

About the Contributors

WARREN G. BENNIS is a Distinguished Professor of Business Administration at the University of Southern California in Los Angeles. He also serves as the Thomas S. Murphy Distinguished Research Scholar at Harvard Business School in Boston and as Chair of the Advisory Board of the Kennedy School's Center for Public Leadership at Harvard University in Cambridge, Massachusetts. He is the author of more than 25 books on leadership and change.

DIANE L. COUTU, dcoutu@hbsp.harvard.edu, is a Senior Editor at HBR specializing in psychology and business.

DANIEL GOLEMAN is the author of *Emotional Intelligence* and coauthor of *Primal Leadership: Realizing the Power of Emotional Intelligence*. He is the co-Chairman of the Consortium for Research on Emotional Intelligence in Organizations, which is based at Rutgers University's Graduate School of Applied and Professional Psychology in Piscataway, New Jersey. He can be reached at Daniel.Goleman@verizon.net.

BARBARA KELLERMAN is the Research Director of the Center for Public Leadership and a lecturer in public policy at Harvard's John F. Kennedy School of Government in Cambridge, Massachusetts. Formerly the Director of the Center for the Advance Study of Leadership at the University of

Maryland, she has written and edited many books on leadership, including her forthcoming *Bad Leadership*.

MICHAEL MACCOBY is an anthropologist and a psychoanalyst. He is also the Founder and President of the Maccoby Group, a management consultancy in Washington, D.C., and was formerly Director of the Program on Technology, Public Policy, and Human Development at Harvard University's Kennedy School of Government in Cambridge, Massachusetts. This article was the basis for the book *The Productive Narcissist: The Promise and Peril of Visionary Leadership*.

LYNN R. OFFERMANN is a professor of organizational sciences and psychology at George Washington University in Washington, D.C., and the Director of the university's doctoral program in industrial and organizational psychology. She can be reached at lro@gwu.edu.

W.C.H. PRENTICE was formerly the President of Bryant and Stratton Business Institutes in Buffalo, New York, the President of Wheaton College in Norton, Massachusetts, and the Dean of Swarthmore College in Swarthmore, Pennsylvania. He is now retired.

ABRAHAM ZALEZNIK is the Konosuke Matsushita Professor of Leadership Emeritus at Harvard Business School in Boston.

Index